The
Odd-Ball Knitting
Book

The Odd-Ball Knitting Book

DEBBY ROBINSON

ST. MARTIN'S PRESS

Library of Congress catalog card number: 88–42958

ISBN 0–312–02452–5

First published 1988 by Bloomsbury Publishing Limited, 2, Soho Square, London W1V 5DE, UK.

First U.S. Edition

10 9 8 7 6 5 4 3 2 1

Produced by the Justin Knowles Publishing Group, 9 Colleton Crescent, Exeter EX2 4BY, UK

Printed and bound by New Interlitho

Contents

Introduction

As the title of this book clearly suggests, the patterns that follow are specifically designed to use up your odd balls of yarn. Most knitters accumulate odd amounts as a result either of abandoned projects or of sale bargains or, most commonly, as a result of excess buying. All commercially produced knitting patterns calculate the amount of yarn that is required and round up the amounts – usually to the nearest ounce – depending on the weight of the yarn that is being used. In addition, allowance must be made for yarn wastage when new balls are joined in and for sewing up. The materials that are quoted are, therefore, by necessity on the generous side to ensure that you do not run out of yarn before the garment is finished. You should avoid running out of yarn if at all possible because the availability of any yarn cannot be guaranteed and the dye lots always vary, so that matching a yarn after the first batch has been purchased may prove impossible.

As a result of this over-estimation of the quantity of yarn required, knitters are often left with unnecessarily large amounts of wool. For instance, if a garment knitted in three colors requires a fraction under 9oz each, the amounts given in the pattern will have to be rounded up at least 1oz to ensure that you will have a sufficient amount. You may then find that you have three whole balls left over. If you are lucky enough to have a friendly yarn store which is prepared to take back left-overs, you have no problem, but if you do not, the following will provide useful information on how to use up the odd balls.

Most of the odd-ball patterns which follow require a maximum of 1¾oz of each color – some require less and a few require 3½oz. It is intended that the patterns will enable you to use up your odd skeins of yarn without having to buy additional amounts. If sale bargains are available, however, you should take advantage of them, especially if the yarns are compatible with any that you already have, because this will give you a larger choice of possibilities when you come to combine colors and textures to the best artistic effect.

Many of the patterns, such as the Textured Stitch Sweater on page 46, leave the choice of color and texture quantities to you, provided that you have the total requirement before you start and you use your own judgement to distribute the different colors and textures evenly throughout the garment – i.e., if you use all your favorite yarns on the body, when you come to work the sleeves you will find that you are left with the ones which you do not like and which do not go together anyway. Here must be included an important word of warning: you should never use up odd balls simply for the sake of doing so. If you have a cupboard full of abandoned balls of green yarn for instance, it probably indicates that you and your family don't like wearing green, and if you knit a garment with these odd balls, it will probably remain in the cupboard forever. You should take as much care planning color schemes which use odd balls as you take when knitting a regular pattern – in fact, greater care is required, as the combinations will usually be, by necessity, limited.

Before you start an odd-ball pattern, you should weigh the yarns carefully if they are not in complete balls and ensure that you have the full amount that has been quoted because the quantities have been carefully estimated to avoid generating even more odd balls. Some of the patterns include helpful tips in cases where you might have a difficulty, such as how to work sock toes in a contrasting shade if you run out of the main shade. As a general rule, however, it is not worth taking a chance with smaller quantities because different brands of yarn and even different dyes will affect the yardage of a yarn – i.e., how far a particular weight will actually go.

On the subject of weight, it should be remembered that all of the patterns, with the exception of the Children's Striped Sweater on page 53, have used natural fibers, so that if the materials quote worsted weight wool, it means 100 per cent wool. If you are using yarn with a synthetic-fiber content, the same weight of yarn will invariably go further, with yarns such as high-bulk acrylics going almost twice as far as pure wools of the equivalent thickness. The mohair that was used for all of the samples was 78 per cent mohair, 13 per cent wool and 9 per cent nylon, which is a fairly standard mix, pure mohair being rare. If you consider substituting a heavier yarn, such as heavy weight worsted wool instead of mohair (these will, in fact, produce the same gauge and are therefore theoretically interchangeable), do allow extra since the amount quoted in the pattern will definitely be short of your requirements.

For patterns where the specific choice of yarn is left to you, do not assume that this means that you may ignore the gauge specification. Gauge must always be accurate, as explained on page 8.

Abbreviations

alt	alternate(ly)
beg	begin(ning)
cont	continue/continuing
dec	decrease/decreasing
in	inch(es)
inc	increase/increasing
k	knit
kb1	knit 1 into back of st
LH	left hand
m1	make one – i.e., inc 1 st by working into the st below the next st to be worked on the left-hand needle, then into the stitch itself
p	purl
psso	pass slipped stitch over
rep	repeat
rev st st	reverse st st
RH	right hand
RS	right side
sl	slip
st(s)	stitch(es)
st st	stocking stitch
tbl	through back of loop(s)
tog	together
WS	wrong side
yb	yarn back
yf	yarn forward
yo	yarn over needle (to create a new st)

Techniques

GAUGE

Knitting is simply the process of making a series of interconnecting loops, the formation of which is completely under the knitter's control. Gauge is the term used to describe the actual stitch size – its width regulating the stitch gauge measurement, and its depth regulating the row gauge measurement. Obtaining a particular gauge is not a magical skill, denied to all but the initiated. It is a technicality, the controlling factor of which is the size of needles used by the knitter.

Since all knitting instructions are drafted to size using mathematical calculations that relate to one gauge and one gauge only, you must achieve the stated gauge before you start work or you will have no control over the size of the finished garment. *This is the most important rule of knitting.*

At the beginning of every pattern a gauge measurement is given, using a specific stitch and needle size – e.g., "using No.8 needles and measured over st st, 18 sts and 24 rows = 4in square". You must work a gauge sample using the same stitch and needle size as quoted. Cast on the appropriate number of stitches plus at least two extra, because edge stitches do not give an accurate measurement. When it is complete, lay the gauge sample or swatch on a flat surface and, taking great care not to squash or stretch it, measure

the gauge, using a ruler and pins as shown.

If there are too few stitches, your gauge is too loose. Use needles that are one size smaller to work another swatch. If there are too many stitches, your gauge is too tight. Use needles that are one size larger to work another swatch.

Even if you have to change needle sizes several times, *keep working swatches until you get it right*. You save no time by skipping this stage of the work; if you do not get the correct gauge, you risk having to undo an entire garment that has worked out to the wrong size.

You may feel that a slight difference is negligible, but a gauge measurement that is only a fraction of a stitch out in every inch will result in the garment being the wrong size, since each fraction will be multiplied by the number of inches across the work.

If you have to change your needle size to achieve the correct gauge for the main stitch, remember to adjust, in ratio, the needles used for other parts of the garment that are worked on different sized needles. For example, if you are using one size smaller needles than are quoted for stockinette stitch, use one size smaller needles than are quoted for the ribs.

Many people worry unnecessarily about row gauge, changing their needle size even though they have achieved the correct stitch gauge. Although important, row gauge does vary considerably from yarn to yarn and from knitter to knitter. If your stitch gauge is absolutely accurate, your row gauge will be only slightly out. Nevertheless, keep an eye on your work, especially when working something like a sleeve that has been calculated in rows rather than inches, and compare it with the measurement chart in case it is noticeably longer or shorter.

The fairisle method of color knitting can make a great deal of difference to your gauge. If you are working a motif in fairisle on a one-color background, take extra care with the gauge, working as loosely as possible so that the motif area does not pull more tightly than the stitches around it, so causing your work to pucker

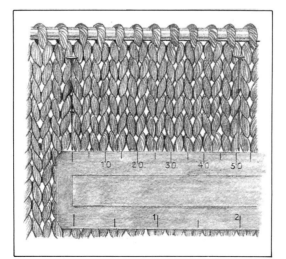

Measuring gauge precisely

and the actual motif to become distorted. To avoid this, it is advisable to use the intarsia method wherever practicable (*see* page 10).

TURNING

Turning is also sometimes called "working short rows", since this is precisely what is done. By turning the work mid-row and leaving part of it unworked, your piece of knitting is shaped, because one side has more rows than the other. If the work is then bound off, the edge will slope, and this is, therefore, an ideal way to shape shoulders. Turning is not advisable if you are working complicated stitches or color patterns, because the process of turning is likely to throw them out.

Unfortunately, holes tend to form at the turning points, even if care is taken. There is a way of overcoming this, and, although it appears complicated at first, it is well worth the effort of learning to master the technique. The method may be used on right or wrong side rows; here it is illustrated on the right side of stockinette stitch.

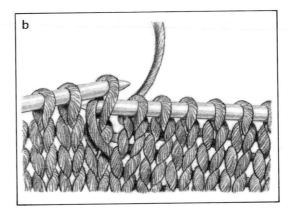

by putting the yarn forward and then back as above. Then:

1. Slip this stitch from the left-hand to the right-hand needle.

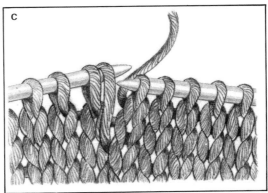

2. Using the point of the left-hand needle, lift the loop up on to the right-hand needle, making an extra stitch.
3. Replace the two stitches on to the left-hand needle, making sure that they are not twisted, and knit them together.

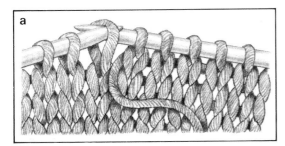

1. Knit to the point where turning is indicated, but before doing so bring the yarn to the front of the work and slip the next stitch from the left-hand to the right-hand needle.
2. Put the yarn to the back of the work and return the slipped stitch to the left-hand needle.
3. Now turn the work and purl to the end.

Repeat the last three steps at every turning point. All the stitches must now be worked across, and so if the turned shaping is being worked immediately before binding off or knitting a seam, you should add an extra row. Work to the first stitch that has had a loop made around it

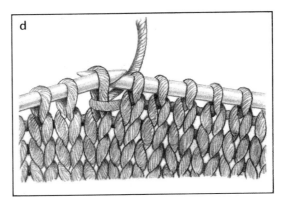

Work to the next "looped" stitch and repeat the process. When this row is completed, the work may be continued as normal.

a
Knit to the point where turning is indicated, but, before doing so, bring the yarn to the front of the work and slip the next stitch from the left-hand to the right-hand needle.

b
Put the yarn to the back of the work and return the slipped stitch to the left-hand needle.

c
Slip this stitch from the left-hand to the right-hand needle, lifting the strand of the loop on to the right-hand needle together with the stitch.

d
Slip both the strand and the stitch back to the left-hand needle, straightening them as you do so.

9

INTARSIA

Intarsia is the term used to describe the technique of color knitting by which each separate area of color is worked using a separate ball of yarn. The colors are not carried from one area to another as with fairisle knitting. Any design that involves large blocks of isolated color that are not going to be repeated along a row or required again a few rows later should be worked in this way.

There is no limit to the number of colors that may be used on any one row, other than that imposed by lack of patience or dexterity. Apart from the problem of getting into a tangle if there are too many separate balls of yarn hanging from the back of your work, you should also remember that every time a new ball of yarn is introduced and broken off after use, two extra ends are produced that will have to be secured when you are finishing the garment. When ends are left, always make sure that they are long enough to thread up so that they may be properly fastened off with a pointed tapestry needle. Do this carefully through the backs of the worked stitches so that the design on the right side of the work is not distorted. On no account should you knot the ends to secure them; as well as looking unsightly, the knots will invariably work themselves loose.

If only a few large, regular areas of color are being worked, the different balls of yarn may be laid on a table in front of you while you work or kept separate in individual jam jars or even shoe boxes. This stops the wool getting into a tangle but requires careful turning at the end of every row so that the yarns do not become twisted.

The easiest method is to use small bobbins that hold each color separately and hang at the back of the work. These may be bought from most large yarn stores or made at home out of stiff cardboard. They come in a variety of shapes, but all have a narrow slit in them to keep the wound yarn in place but allow the knitter to unwind a controlled amount as and when required. When winding yarn on to a bobbin, try to wind sufficient to complete an entire area of color but don't overwind, as heavy bobbins will pull stitches out of shape.

When you change color from one stitch to another, it is vital that you twist the yarns around each other before dropping the old color and working the first stitch in the new color. This prevents a hole forming. If you do not twist the yarns there is no strand to connect the last stitch worked in color A to the first stitch worked in color B. Twist the yarns quite firmly to prevent a gap appearing after the work has settled.

FAIRISLE

Colorful fairisles are *the* classic look of British knitting and are the ideal way to use up odd balls of yarn. Since the charted pattern is a regulated repeat and not a random use of color as found elsewhere in this book, it is very important to weigh your yarns carefully so that you do not run out before you have completed your garment. The amounts quoted within the patterns have been rounded up to ensure that this does not happen. When you are using the fairisle method of knitting, a double fabric is produced because one color is being carried behind the other all

Yarns on bobbins showing how the two colors are twisted on the wrong side (WS) of the work.

the time, so lighter weight yarns are preferable.

The planning of the colorway is extremely important and well worth taking considerable care over. It is sometimes necessary to knit several test swatches before you achieve the right combination because knitting a test piece first is the only way to create an accurate idea of the finished garment. A colorful array of balls of wool may appear very attractive when they are laid out on the table, but once they are knitted, they may combine disastrously. Colors do, in fact, interact with one another in a very subtle and often unexpected way, depending on how they are combined and in what ratio.

Keep an open mind when you combine colors because there are no strict rules governing how well one color will work with another because it is the effect of the whole that is important rather than the individual colors which have created the effect. In this respect, it is similar to an artist's palette of paints which may be combined to form new colors when they are applied to the canvas.

When you knit a fairly small-scale pattern, as in the patterns on pages 38 and 46, it is important to choose colors that are tonally similar – i.e., if most of your colors are in the mid-range of intensity, do not use odd ones that are very light, dark or bright, because these will tend to stand out from the rest of the design. The ideal mix is a balance between intense and less intense colors, because if you use colors of similar tones the pattern will not have any definition. A choice of colors of different tones can make the same basic pattern look quite different, as the examples that have been photographed illustrate.

The technique of color knitting called "fairisle" is often confused with the traditional style of color knitting that originated in the Fair Isles and took its name from those islands. Instructions that call for the fairisle method do not necessarily produce the multi-colored, geometric patterns that are associated with the Fair Isle style of knitting. The technique is suitable for any style of work in which small repetitive areas of color make the use of individual balls of yarn (intarsia method), impracticable.

Fairisle may be defined as knitting in which two colors are used across a row, the one not in use being carried at the back of the work until it is next required. This is normally done by dropping one color and picking up the other with your right hand. If you are lucky enough to have mastered both the "English" and "Continental" methods of knitting, both hands may be used so that neither yarn has to be dropped. One color is held in the left hand while the other color is held in the right hand at all times. The instructions below, however, cover the more standard one-handed method and give the three alternative ways of dealing with the yarn not in use.

Stranding
Stranding is the term used to describe the technique by which the yarn not in use is simply left hanging at the back of the work until it is next needed. The yarn in use is then dropped and the carried yarn taken up, ready for action. This means that the strand or "float" produced on the wrong side of the work pulls directly on the stitches on either side of it.

It is essential that the float is long enough to span the gap without pulling stitches out of shape and to allow the stitches in front of it to stretch and prevent them from puckering on the right side of the work. It is preferable to go to the other extreme and to leave a small loop at the back of the work rather than pulling the float too tightly.

If the gap to be bridged by the float is wide, the strands produced may easily be caught and pulled when the garment is put on or taken off. This may be remedied by catching the floats down with a few stitches on the wrong side of the work when you are finishing off the garment.

Weaving
With weaving, the yarn being carried is looped over or under the working yarn on every stitch, creating an up and down woven effect on the wrong side of the

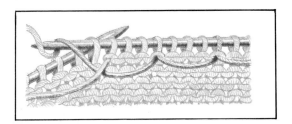

The "floats" created by stranding at the correct gauge.

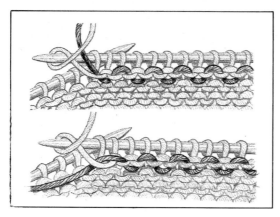

work. Since the knitter does not have to gauge the length of the floats, many people find that this is the easiest method of ensuring an even, accurate gauge. Weaving does increase the chances of the carried color showing through on to the right side of the work, however, and it tends to produce a far denser fabric, which is not always desirable, especially if a thick, warm fiber such as mohair is being used.

Stranding and weaving

Combining the two methods of stranding and weaving is invariably the most practicable solution to the problem of working perfect fairisle. Most designs have color areas that contain varying numbers of stitches. If the gap between areas of the same color is only a few stitches, then stranding will suffice, but if the float produced will be too long, weave the carried yarn in every few stitches. Should you be unsure about the length of float to leave, slip your fingers under one: if you succeed with ease, the float is too long.

The most difficult aspect of fairisle knitting is to get the gauge correct. This does not depend on the stitch size so much as on the way you treat the carried yarn. This is why, when you work an all-over fairisle pattern, you should always knit a gauge sample in fairisle, not in base color stockinette stitch, because the weaving or stranding will greatly affect the finished measurement of the stitches.

The most important rule to remember is that *the yarn being carried must be woven or stranded loosely enough to have the same degree of "give" as the knitting itself.* Unless you achieve this, the resulting fabric will have no elasticity whatsoever, and very tight floats will buckle the stitches so that they lie badly on the right side of the work. On complicated designs, when more than two colors are used on a row, it may be necessary to carry more than one yarn at the back of the work. This should be avoided if at all possible, because ensuring that each color is woven in at the correct place is time consuming and results in an even heavier fabric. In such instances it may be advisable to combine the methods of intarsia and fairisle.

SEAMS

After achieving the correct gauge, the most important technique to master is the final sewing up of your knitting. This can make or break a garment, however carefully it may have been knitted, and is the reason the making up instructions in every knitting pattern should be followed precisely, especially the type of seam to be used and the order in which the seams are to be worked.

Before starting any piece of work always leave an end of yarn that will be long enough to complete a substantial part of the eventual seam, if not the whole thing. When you have worked a couple of rows, wind the end up and pin it to the work to keep it out of the way. If necessary, also leave a sizeable end when the work has been completed so that you may use it for seaming rather than joining in a new end, which may well work loose, especially at stress points such as welts.

The secret of perfect-looking seams is uniformity and regularity of stitch. When you join two pieces that have been worked in the same stitch they should be joined row for row. All work should be pinned first to ensure that the fabric is evenly distributed. When joining work that has a design on both pieces, take great care to match the colors, changing the color you are using to sew the seam where necessary.

Backstitch

Pin the two pieces of work together, right sides facing, and make sure that the edges are absolutely flush. Always leave as narrow a seam allowance as possible to reduce unnecessary bulk. It is essential that the line of backstitches is kept straight and you should use the lines of the knitted stitches as a guide. All the stitches should be the same length, one starting immediately after the previous one has finished. The stitches should form a continuous straight line on the side of the work facing you. If the seam starts at the very edge of the work, close the edges with an overcast stitch, as shown, before working the backstitch:

1. Make a running stitch (maximum length ½in), through both thicknesses of work.

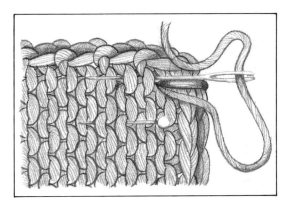

2. Put the needle back into the work in exactly the same spot as before and make another running stitch, twice as long as the first.

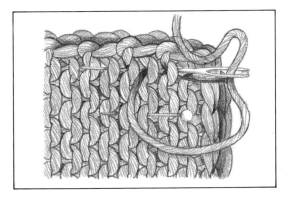

3. Put the needle back into the work at the same point at which the previous stitch ended. Make another stitch, the same length.

Keep repeating step 3 until you reach the last stitch, which should be half as long as the other stitches to fill in the gap left at the end of the seam.

By keeping the stitch line straight and by pulling the yarn fairly firmly after each stitch, no gaps should appear when the work is opened out and the seam pulled apart.

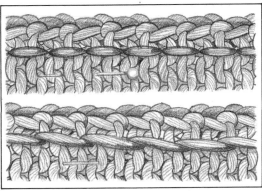

This seam is suitable for lightweight yarns or where an untidy selvedge has been worked.

Flat seam
The expression "flat seam" is a slight contradiction in terms since it involves an oversewing action. However, when the work is opened out it will do so completely and lie quite flat, unlike a backstitched seam.

Use a blunt-ended tapestry needle to avoid splitting the knitted stitches. After pinning both pieces, right sides together, hold the work as shown. Pass the needle through the very edge stitch on the back piece and then through the very edge stitch on the front piece. Pull the yarn through and repeat the action, placing the needle through exactly the same part of each stitch every time. Always work through the edge stitch only. If you take in more than this, you will have a lumpy, untidy seam that will never lie flat.

When two pieces of stockinette stitch are to be joined with a flat seam, do not work a special selvedge (such as knitting every edge stitch). Work the edge stitches normally but as tightly as possible, using the very tip of your needle. When you come to work the seam, place the tapestry needle behind the knots of the edge stitches and not through the looser strands that run between the knots, for these will not provide a firm enough base for the seam, which will appear gappy when opened out.

Flat seams are essential for garments made of heavy-weight yarns on which a backstitch would create far too much bulk. They should also be used for attaching buttonbands, collars and so forth, when flatness and neatness are essential. Borders, waistbands, cuffs and

Top: the line of backstitch facing you. Below: the line of backstitch on the other side of the work.

Make a running stitch through both thicknesses of work.

Put the needle back into the work in exactly the same place as before and make another running stitch twice as long as the first.

13

any other part of the garment where the edge of the seam will be visible should also be joined with a flat seam, even if the remainder of the garment has backstitched seams. In these instances, start with a flat seam until the rib/border is complete and then change over to backstitch, taking in a tiny seam allowance at first and then smoothly widening it, making sure that you do not suddenly increase the depth of the seam.

Sewn slip stitch

If one piece of work is to be placed on top of another – for example, when turning in a double neckband, folding over a hem or attaching the edges of pocket borders – you should use a slip stitch.

When you are turning in a neckband that has been bound off, place the needle through the bound-off edge and then through the appropriate stitch on the row where it was initially knitted up. It is essential that you follow the line of the stitch to avoid twisting the neckband. As you repeat the action, the visible sewn stitch runs at a diagonal.

The same rule applies when you sew down a neckband that has not been bound off but on which the stitches are held on a thread. The only difference is that the needle is placed through the actual held stitch to secure it. When each stitch has been slip-stitched down, the thread may be removed. This method results in a neckband with more "give" in it than one that has been bound off.

When you are slip-stitching a turned-in waistband, use the line of a row as a guide to produce a perfectly straight, horizontal line of stitches, which should not show through to the right side of the work. On pocket borders, use the line of stitches on the main work as a guide to produce a perfectly straight vertical line of stitches. Pass the tapestry needle through one

Top: working a flat seam. Below: a flat seam on the right side (RS) of the work.

Right:
Working a sewn slip stitch.

Far Right:
A turned neckband being stitched down through non-bound-off stitches.

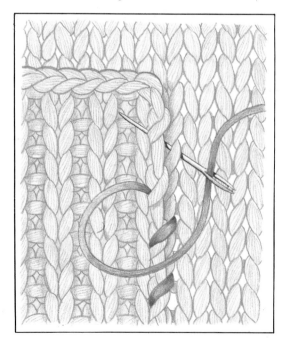

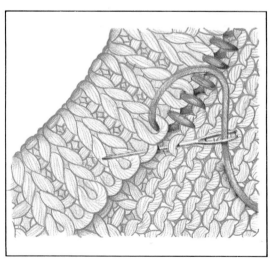

strand of the main work stitch and then
behind the knot of the border edge stitch,
as for a flat seam.

KNITTED SEAMS

This method of joining is perfect for
shoulders on which no shaping has been
worked or on which the shaping has been
worked by turning rows (*see* page 9). It
creates an extremely neat, flat seam.

   Because the two pieces to be joined
must be worked stitch for stitch, they must
both have exactly the same number of
stitches. Even though the pattern will
specify that you should have a certain
number of stitches on your needles at this
point, it is wise to double check the
number you actually have, as it is very
easy to lose or gain a stitch accidentally as
you work.

   The technique itself requires three
needles. The stitches from the front and
back are held on their respective needles,
which should both be in your left hand,
while in your right hand you should hold
a third needle. This third needle should be
larger than the others to help prevent the
bound-off stitches being too tight.
Holding more than one needle in the hand
and trying to work through two stitches at
a time without dropping them can seem
very awkward at first, but, with a little
practice, it will feel like normal knitting.
Hold the needles so that the right sides of
the work face one another and so that the
stitches line up at corresponding intervals
on the front and back needles. Work as
follows:

1. The point of the right-hand needle is
   put through the first stitch on the front
   needle and the first stitch on the back
   needle, with exactly the same action as
   a regular knit stitch but going through
   both simultaneously.

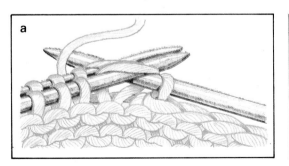

2. Pull a loop through to form a single
   stitch on the right-hand needle,
   slipping the old stitches off the left-
   hand needles.

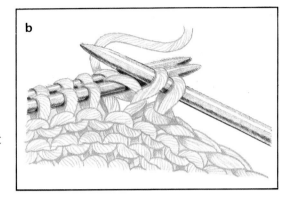

3. Repeat steps 1 and 2 so that there are
   two stitches on the right-hand needle.
   The second stitch is then lifted over the
   first, as in regular binding off.

Step 3 should be repeated across all the
stitches to be knitted together until one
loop remains on the right-hand needle.
Pull the yarn through this to secure it.

   When you are knitting together a
shoulder seam on a garment on which no
neck shaping has been worked and on
which the neck stitches have not been
bound off, all the stitches on the back may
be dealt with at the same time. Start to
work the first shoulder together from the
armhole to the neck edge, then bind off
the back neck (if the pattern requires that
they are bound off), without breaking the
yarn, which may then be used to knit
together the second shoulder seam from
neck to armhole.

   Although it is normally worked on the
inside of the work to create an extremely
neat, flat and durable seam, a knitted
seam may also be worked with the wrong
sides of the knitting facing one another.
This creates a decorative ridge on the
right side of the work.

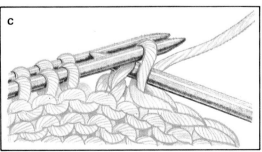

a
*The point of the right-hand
needle is put through the
first stitch on the front
needle and the first stitch on
the back needle, with
exactly the same action as a
normal knit stitch but going
through both at the same
time.*

b
*Repeat the first two steps so
that there are two stitches
on the right-hand needle.*

c
*The second stitch is lifted
over the first, as in normal
binding off.*

KNITTING UP STITCHES

The term "picking up" stitches is sometimes used instead of "knitting up" stitches, but it is rather a misleading phrase since it implies that the stitches are simply strands that have been pulled out around the edge of the work. This should never be done, for it produces uneven and untidy loops. The correct method is to use new yarn to create brand new stitches through the edge of the existing knitted fabric. This produces neat, uniform stitches, and allows you to control the positioning of them.

As with working perfect flat seams, the preparation – i.e., the actual knitting – is the most important part of knitting up stitches. A firmly and neatly worked edge is essential for neat knitting up of stitches. Always work edge stitches tightly, and if shaping has been worked – around a neckline, for instance – any decreases or increases should be worked one or two stitches in from the edge stitch wherever the pattern will allow. In this way the irregular, stretched stitches of the shaping are out of the way and the normally worked edge stitches can form the basis of the new stitches. Each new stitch should emerge from behind the knot of the edge stitch as this is the firmest part of the stitch. The strand between the knots will tend to stretch and should be used only when there is no alternative.

If you are working a color pattern on a main color, stop the pattern short a few stitches in from the edge so that the last few stitches are worked in main color only. Knitting up from stitches of various colors will create an untidy line. When you are completing a piece of work that is to have stitches knitted up at a later stage, leave the yarn attached so that it may be used when required and so that you do not have to join in a new end of yarn, which will have to be secured.

When a pattern states exactly how many stitches are to be knitted up, if you are to work them in a stitch for which you have not worked a separate gauge sample – e.g., rib when the pattern has required you to work a gauge sample over stock-inette stitch – it is worthwhile to work a few knitted up stitches as a test before beginning the actual knitting, since rib gauge varies compared with stockinette stitch.

If you find it difficult to distribute the number of stitches that are to be knitted up, divide your work into halves and then into quarters (and even eighths if it is a long edge), and mark these points with pins. Divide the number of stitches equally among these sections. If they do not divide equally, use any extra stitches where they might be needed, such as at seam edges. Never distribute the stitches as you go along as this will invariably result in an uneven effect, with some areas bunched with too many stitches and others stretched with too few.

Once the edge has been prepared, hold the work with the right side towards you. Hold the yarn at the back of the work so that the stitches may be pulled through to the front. This may be done either with the needle you intend to use for the first row or, more easily, with a crochet hook. Use a crochet hook that will slip easily through the base stitch to catch the yarn and pull it through to the right side of the work where it is then slipped on to the needle holding the new stitches. Pull the yarn tight. The holding needle should be one or two sizes smaller than the size quoted for the actual knitting up to reduce the stitch size on the first row, thus creating a neater finish. Change to the correct needle size on your second row. The first row of a band or border that is to be ribbed may also be either knitted or purled as this, too, creates a smaller stitch than an initial row of ribbing. Knitting this row with the right side facing you gives a smooth, inconspicuous row. If you purl this row, a ridge will be formed on the right side of the work, which will neaten the knit-up edge in a more ornamental way. Ribbing should then continue as normal.

If stitches are held between two areas of knitted-up stitches, as they may often be at the center front edge of a crew neck, slip these stitches on to another needle and then knit them on to the holding needle. This will save you from having to break the yarn; slip the held stitches on to the holding needle and join in the yarn again to knit up further stitches. It is also advisable to knit up a stitch from the loop at the beginning and the end of any set of stitches that have been bound off or are on a holder. These are stress points and often become stretched, and an extra stitch will prevent a hole forming.

If you are using a set of double-pointed needles to knit around some necklines, the same rules apply, but the stitches that are knitted up must be equally distributed among the number of needles in use, leaving one needle free for working.

SECURING THE ENDS

Because many of the odd-ball patterns include numerous yarns, which are often worked in small areas, the number of ends they produce may appear daunting, but these may be dealt with efficiently in one of two ways.

First, minimize the number of times that you cut the yarn and join in a new one by carrying the yarn not in use up the side of the work wherever this is feasible – i.e., where doing so will not create a serious tangle. You should never join a new yarn part way across a row if it can be joined in at the very beginning of that row. Watch your yarn at all times so that you can anticipate the next join.

Where yarns must be joined within the work, for instance when working the Patchwork Raglan Sweater on page 30, leave a good sized end so that it may be secured at a later stage by threading up a pointed tapestry needle and working through the backs of a few self-colored stitches and then back through itself. Take care that this does not show through on the right side of the work and also that it does not distort the stitches by being pulled through them too tightly. Do not knot the ends as this creates an unsightly reverse side, and the ends will eventually work loose, causing gaps and dropped stitches.

On the styles where the yarns are joined in at the sides of the work, loosely knot the old yarn with the new so that the two ends will not cause the edge stitches to work loose, and leave at least 1½in before you cut them.

With all the ends forming a fringe along the edges of the work, they may be secured quickly and permanently. If you have a sewing-machine that will take knitted fabric, the best method is to run a line of fairly small machine stitches along the very edge of the work. Smooth out the ends at right angles to the work, then fold them back over it and catch them down in this position. They may then be trimmed close to the work because the machine stitching will hold them secure.

If you prefer to secure the ends by hand, you may do this at the seaming stage. This can be done most neatly when backstitch is worked with a pointed tapestry needle. The ends can be caught down under the line of the backstitch, and you should put the point of the needle through the ends as you work. The only drawback with this method is that if you have numerous ends to secure, the finished seam will be rather bulky.

You should never cut corners where ends are concerned, however tempting it may be just to snip off a stray end with your scissors. It is far easier to thread a needle and secure the end immediately than it is to have to make an obvious repair at a later date when the damage has already been done.

EMBROIDERY

Satin stitch
Satin stitch is used to "fill-in" areas such as rabbits' noses. It is formed by working straight stitches, very close to one another, over the length of the area to be covered.

Backstitch
Backstitch should be worked in exactly the same way as the stitch used for seams (*see* p 13). When you are working a curve, try to make very small stitches to ensure a continuous line.

Entrelac Jacket

Materials

Mohair with a low synthetic content: total weight required is 23oz.
NOTE: Each piece of entrelac weighs less than ¼oz, therefore small amounts may be used provided you have the total amount required. Allow 1¾oz of one color for the edging and collar.

Needles

One pair of No.7 and one pair of No.8 needles.

Gauge

Using No.8 needles and measured over st st, 18 sts = 4in.

The clever way that the method of entrelac knitting "weaves" areas of color means that even the tiniest scraps of yarn may be used to make this edge-to-edge, mandarin-collared jacket. The sample has been worked in rich jewel tones of mohair – the perfect garment for the evening. The jacket is drop-shouldered and has bracelet-length sleeves.

If you have not worked in entrelac before, the instructions may seem strange at first. It is a good idea, therefore, to study the diagram to see the direction in which you will be knitting at any given point, the RS being shown facing you.

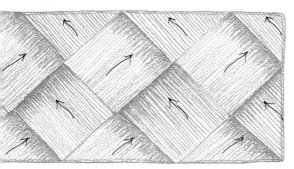

A diagram of a piece of entrelac knitting showing the direction of working.

Back

Using edging color and No.8 needles, cast on 80 sts. Throughout the entrelac, change color at random when each individual triangle or rectangle is started.

Form base triangles.

Row 1(WS): using first color, p2, turn.
Row 2: k2, turn.
Row 3: p3 (purling the extra st from the LH needle), turn.
Row 4: k3, turn.
Row 5: p4, turn.
Row 6: k4, turn.
Cont in pattern as established, adding an extra st on every purl row until there are 8 sts on the RH needle, ending with a purl row. This forms one triangle. Work 9 more triangles in the same way so that all 80 sts are now on the RH needle.

*Work selvedge triangle.

Row 1: k2, turn.
Row 2: p2, turn.
Row 3: inc into the first st, sl 1, k1, psso, turn.
Row 4: p3, turn.
Row 5: k1, inc into next st, sl 1, k1, psso, turn.

Row 6: p4, turn.
Row 7: k1, inc into next st, k1, sl 1, k1, psso, turn.
Row 8: p5, turn.
Row 9: k1, inc into next st, k2, sl 1, k1, psso, turn.
Cont in pattern as established, inc into the 2nd st on every k row until you have 8 sts, ending with a k row.
Work the first rectangle: this is knitted up from the second side of the first base triangle (*see* diagram for direction of knitting).
Knit up 8 sts along this edge, working from top to bottom with the RS facing.
Row 1: p8, turn.
Row 2: k7, sl 1, k next st from LH needle, psso, turn.
Keep repeating the last 2 rows until all the sts from the first side of the second triangle have been incorporated. This completes the first rectangle. Work a rectangle from the 8 following triangles, then, from the second side of the last triangle, **form a selvedge triangle:**
Knit up 8 sts as from the previous triangles.
Row 1: p2 tog, p6, turn.
Row 2: k7.
Row 3: p2 tog, p5, turn.
Cont in pattern, until 1 st remains, fasten off.
Another line of rectangles is now worked in the opposite direction, starting by knitting up 8 sts from the bottom to the top along the inner edge of the selvedge triangle which has just been worked, with RS facing.
Row 1: p7, p2 tog (1 st from triangle, 1 st from rectangle).
Row 2: k8.
Keep repeating the last 2 rows until all the sts from the rectangle have been incorporated. Work the remaining rectangles as established, finishing by incorporating the sts from the selvedge triangle at the end.*
Rep from * to * 7 times more. To finish with a straight edge, form a row of triangles.
Row 1: k2, turn.
Row 2: p2, turn.
Row 3: inc into first st, sl 1, k1, psso, turn.
Row 4: p3, turn.
Row 5: k1, inc into next st, sl 1, k1, psso, turn.
Row 6: p4, turn.
Row 7: k1, inc into next st, k1, sl 1, k1,

psso, turn.
Row 8: p5, turn.
Row 9: k2 tog, k2, sl 1, k1, psso, turn.
Row 10: p4, turn.
Row 11: k2 tog, k1, sl 1, k1, psso, turn.
Row 12: p3, turn.
Row 13: k2 tog, sl 1, k1, psso, turn.
Row 14: p2 tog, turn. Slip this st to RH needle and then knit up 8 sts along the second side of the first rectangle from the top to the bottom, with RS facing.
Row 1: p7, p2 tog.
Row 2: sl 1, k1, psso, k5, sl 1, k1 (from next rectangle), psso, turn.
Row 3: p7.
Row 4: sl 1, k1, psso, k4, sl 1, k1, psso, turn.
Row 5: p6.
Cont in pattern until you are purling 2 sts only.
Next row: k1, sl 1, k1, psso, k1, turn.
Next row: sl 1, k2 tog, psso.
Work from the next 8 rectangles in the same manner and finish with another triangle, first knitting up 8 sts from the last rectangle, as before.
Row 1: p7, p2 tog.
Row 2: sl 1, k1, psso, k4, k2 tog.
Row 3: p6.
Row 4: sl 1, k1, psso, k2, k2 tog.
Row 5: p4.
Row 6: sl 1, k1, psso, k2 tog.
Row 7: p2.
Row 8: k2 tog and fasten off.

Right front
Using edge color and No.8 needles, cast on 40 sts. Form 5 base triangles and work as for back until * to * has been worked 7 times in all. **Shape neck** – Work a selvedge triangle as at top edge of back, fastening off the final st left on the needle. Cont to work a normal band of rectangles, finishing with an edge selvedge triangle. Work another band of rectangles in the opposite direction but omit the final one. Turn the work and finish off with triangles as at top of back.

Left front
Rep from * to * 7 times in all and then begin another band of rectangles but instead of working the final rectangle, work the final selvedge triangle as on the top of the back. Work a band of rectangles in the opposite direction omitting to knit up any sts from the first

selvedge triangle and binding off the first rectangle sts. Cont working rectangles normally to end and then work the selvedge triangles as for the top of the back.

Sleeves

Using edge color and No.8 needles, cast on 56 sts. Form 7 base triangles. Work from * to * 4 times in all. Finish with a row of triangles.

Collar

Using edging color and No.7 needles, cast on 80 sts and work in garter st (knit every row), for 2in. Bind off.

Right front edging

Using edging color, No.7 needles and with RS facing, knit up 89 sts (10 sts along each triangle edge plus 1 st at each end and 1 st between each triangle) along the front edge, working from bottom to top. Knit 1 row, then bind off. Work the left front as the right front, but knit up from the top to the bottom.

Finishing

Join shoulder seams with a narrow backstitch.

Using No.7 needles, edging color and with RS facing, knit up 78 sts (distributed as for the right and left fronts) along the top of each sleeve, working from right to left. Knit 1 row. Then knit up 39 sts either side of the shoulder seam in the same manner. Knit 1 row, then knit the sleeve and armhole sts tog (*see* Techniques, page 15). Join side and sleeve seams with a very narrow backstitch and attach the collar to the neck edge by the bound-off edge, using a flat seam.

Sleeveless Fairisle

Women's

Materials
Fingering weight yarn (a Shetland type is ideal, but any yarns of the correct weight may be used): 1¾oz each of 3 colors (including one used for ribs), plus 1oz each of 8 more colors.

Needles
One pair of No.2 and one pair of No.4 needles.

Gauge
Using No.4 needles and measured over fairisle pattern, 32 sts and 1 complete pattern row repeat = 4in.

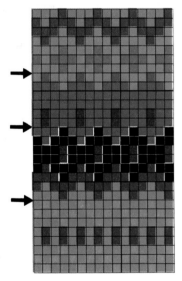

Chart showing Women's Fairisle pattern.
Arrows indicate that 1¾oz wool is required for these colors.

Men's

Materials
Light weight worsted
wool – A, B, C: 3½oz
each; D–I: 1¾oz each; J
and K: 1oz each.

Needles
One pair of No.4 and
one pair of No.6
needles.

Gauge
Using No.6 needles and
measured over fairisle
pattern, 26 sts = 4in.

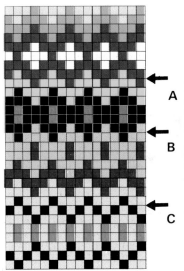

*Chart showing Men's
Fairisle pattern.*

WOMEN'S SLEEVELESS FAIRISLE

Front
Using No.2 needles and rib color, cast on 150 sts.
Row 1 (RS): *k1 tbl, p1, rep from * to end.
Row 2: *k1, p1, rep from * to end.
Keep repeating these 2 rows to form single twisted rib for 2in, ending with a RS row. Next row: purl, inc into every 25th st (156 sts). Change to No.4 needles and start knitting in st st, working the color pattern from the chart. *Keep your floats loose, only weave in every 3-4 sts. The work should have as much "give" as plain st st.* Carry yarns up the side of the work if they are to be used again within a few rows. When work measures 13in, **shape armholes**: bind off 8 sts at beg of next 2 rows. Dec 1 st at each end of every row until 118 sts remain, then dec 1 st at each end of every alt row until 106 sts remain. Work even until piece measures 18¼in, ending with a WS row. **Shape neck**: next row: work pattern over 40 sts, bind off 26 sts, work pattern to end. Cont with this set of sts, leaving the others on a holder. Dec 1 st at neck edge on every row until 25 sts remain. Work this edge even until piece measures 22in, ending with a RS row. **Shape shoulder**: bind off 8 sts at beg of next 2 WS rows. Work 1 row even, then bind these sts off. Return to held sts, join yarn in at neck edge and shape as for other side, reversing shaping.

Back
Work as for front but **shape neck** when work measures 21¼in, ending with a WS row. Next row: work pattern over 29 sts, bind off 48 sts, work pattern to end. Cont with the last set of sts, dec 1 st at neck edge on every row until 25 sts remain. **Shape shoulder**: work as for front. Return to other side of neck and shape as for first side.

Neckband
Sew tog the left shoulder seam using a narrow backstitch. Using No.2 needles, rib color and with RS facing, knit up 4 sts down RS of the back neck, 48 sts across it, 4 sts up the other side. Then knit 26 sts down the left front, 26 sts across it and 26

sts up the other side (134 sts). Purl the first row, then work in single twisted rib for 1in. Bind off loosely.

Right armband
Join the right shoulder seam with a backstitch and the neck edges with a flat seam. Open the work out and, with RS facing, No.2 needles and main color, knit up 150 sts from the back to the front. Purl the first row, then work in single twisted rib for 1in. Bind off loosely.

Left armband
Work as for right armband, but knit up the sts from front to back.

Finishing
Join side seams with a flat seam over the ribs and a backstitch over the pattern.

MEN'S SLEEVELESS FAIRISLE

This man's medium-sized sleeveless sweater will be produced by working the same number of stitches as the fingering weight women's version, but in thicker, light weight worsted wool and using larger needles. The finished chest measurement is 42½in.

Front
Using No.4 needles and rib color, cast on 150 sts.
Row 1 (RS): *k1 tbl, p1, rep from * to end.
Row 2: *k1, p1, rep from * to end.
Keep repeating these 2 rows to form twisted rib for 2in, ending with a RS row. Next row: purl, inc into every 25th st (156 sts). Change to No.6 needles and start working in st st, working the color pattern from the chart. *Keep your floats loose, only weave in every 3–4 sts. The work should have as much "give" as plain st st.* Carry yarns up the side of the work if they are to be used again within a few rows. When work measures 16½in, **shape armholes**: bind off 8 sts at beg of next 2 rows. Dec 1 st at each end of every row until 118 sts remain, then dec 1 st at each end of every alt row until 106 sts remain. Work even until piece measures 22¾in, ending with a WS row. **Shape neck**: next row: work pattern over 40 sts, bind off 26

sts, work pattern to end. Cont with this set of sts, leaving the others on a holder. Dec 1 st at neck edge on every row until 25 sts remain. Work this edge even until work measures 25½in, ending with a RS row. **Shape shoulder**: bind off 8 sts at beg of next 2 WS rows. Work 1 row even, then bind these sts off. Return to held sts, join yarn in at neck edge and shape as for other side, reversing shaping.

Back

Work as for front, but **shape neck** when work measures 24½in, ending with a WS row. Next row: work pattern over 29 sts, bind off 48 sts, work pattern to end. Cont with the last set of sts, dec 1 st at neck edge on every row until 25 sts remain. **Shape shoulder**: work as for front. Return to other side of neck and shape as for first side.

Neckband

Sew tog the left shoulder seam using a narrow backstitch. Using No.4 needles, down RS of the back neck, 48 sts across it, rib color and with RS facing, knit up 4 sts down RS of the back neck, 48 sts across it, 4 sts up the other side. Then knit 28 sts down the left front, 26 sts across it and 28 sts up the other side (138 sts). Purl the first row, then work in single twisted rib for 1in. Bind off loosely.

Right armband

Join the right shoulder seam with a backstitch and the neck edges with a flat seam. Open the work out and, with RS facing, No.4 needles and rib color, knit up 162 sts from the back to the front. Purl the first row, then work in single twisted rib for 1in. Bind off loosely.

Left armband

Work as for right armband, but knit up the sts from front to back.

Finishing

Join side seams with a flat seam over the ribs and a backstitch over the pattern.

Pattern-fronted Waistcoat

Materials
Fingering weight wool –
color for back: 3½oz;
colors A, B, C: 1¾oz
each; color for band:
1¾oz. 5 buttons.

Needles
One pair of No.3, one
pair of No.4 and one
pair of No.6 needles.

Gauge
Using No.4 needles and
measured over st st, 28
sts = 4in.

NOTE: To test the
pattern gauge, use No.6
needles, cast on 18 sts
and work in pattern for
12 rows, then bind off.
From edge to edge,
when completely flat,
this should measure 2in.

A classic waistcoat shape, using fingering weight wool. The fronts are worked in a simple three-color, slip stitch pattern, while the back is knitted in plain stockinette stitch. The bands may be worked in a fifth color or one of the colors used for the main parts, if you have sufficient yarn. Since the stitch and needle sizes are quite different on the fronts and back, you should take particular care when you test the gauges.

Back

Using No.3 needles and back color, cast on 112 sts.
Row 1: *k1, p1, rep from * to end.
Keep repeating this row to form single rib. When rib measures 1in, change to No.4 needles and cont in st st, inc 1 st at each end of next and every following 8th row until you have 128 sts. Work even until piece measures 8½in. **Shape armholes**: bind off 10 sts at beg of next 2 rows. Then dec 1 st at each end of every row until 96 sts remain. Work even until work measures 18¼in. Next RS row: **shape neck**: k27, bind off 42, k to end. Cont with this set of sts, leaving others on a holder. Dec 1 st at neck edge on next 2 rows. **Shape shoulder**: bind off 6 sts at beg of next 3 WS rows, work 1 row even, then bind off remaining sts. Return to held sts, join yarn in at neck edge and shape to match first side.

Pattern

Row 1 (RS): using color B, k1, *yb, sl 2, k2, rep from * to last 3 sts, yb, sl 2, k1.
Row 2: using color B, k1, *yb, sl 1, yf, sl 1, p2, rep from * to last 3 sts, yb, sl 1, yf, sl 1, k1.
Row 3: using color C, k3, *yb, sl 2, k2, rep from *, ending k1.
Row 4: using color C, k1, *p2, yb, sl 1, yf, sl 1, rep from * to last 3 sts, p2, k1.
Rows 5 and 6: using color A, repeat rows 1 and 2.
Rows 7 and 8: using color B, repeat rows 3 and 4.
Rows 9 and 10: using color C, repeat rows 1 and 2.
Rows 11 and 12: using color A, repeat rows 3 and 4.
These 12 rows form the pattern. Take great care when working the edge sts and carrying the yarns up the side so that neat edges are formed when bands are sewn in place.

Right front

(Worked from the shoulder to the lower edge – i.e., upside down.)
Using No.6 needles and color A, cast on 8 sts and purl 1 row. Cast on 8 sts at beg of next row, change to color B and work first row of pattern across these 16 sts. Work row 2.
Row 3: cast on 8 sts, then change to color C and work pattern to end.
Row 4: work pattern to end.
Row 5: cast on 8 sts, then change to color A and work pattern to end (32 sts).
Work 22 rows even. **Shape neck**: inc 1 st at beg of next (WS) row and at this edge on every following 3rd row until there are 60 sts, working all new sts in pattern.
(**NOTE:** If a slip st falls at the end of the row, work it as a knit st.) Work even until work measures 10¼in from beg. **Shape armhole**: inc 1 st at armhole edge on every row until you have 70 sts. Cast on 10 sts at beg of next RS row. Then start dec at this edge, 1 st every 7th row until 66 sts remain. Work even until work measures 7½in from armhole.
Shape front point: dec 1 st on every row on outer edge and on every alt row on inner edge (keeping in pattern as before), until 3 sts remain. Work 1 row. Bind these sts off.

Left front

Work as for right front but knitting the first row that was worked after casting on, starting the pattern on row 2 and reversing all the shapings.

Left band

(First join the shoulder seams using a backstitch.)
Using No.3 needles and color chosen for bands, cast on 8 sts and work in single rib until the band is long enough to fit from the center back neck, down the front to where the bottom "point" shaping starts (when slightly stretched). **Miter the corner**: next row: rib to last 2 sts, turn and rib to end.
Rows 3 and 4: rib to last 4 sts, turn and rib to end.
Rows 5 and 6: rib to last 6 sts, turn and rib to end.
Now rib across all sts and cont in rib to the tip of the point and work another miter, as at first corner. When worked, cont in rib until the band is ½in short of reaching

the side seam edge. Cont in rib, dec 1 st
on the outer edge on every row until 2 sts
remain. Work tog and fasten off. Using
pins, mark position for 5 buttons.

Right band
Work as for left band, reversing the
directions in which the miters are worked
and working a buttonhole to correspond
to each marked button position as follows:
Rib 3, bind off 2, rib 3.
Rib the next row, casting on 2 sts
immediately above those bound off on
previous row.

Armbands
Work as for the buttonband until each is
long enough to reach around the armhole
when very slightly stretched.

Finishing
Join the back, from the end of the rib up,
to the fronts with a backstitch. Join the
cast-on edges of the bands with a flat seam
and pin this at the center of the back neck.
Pin the bound-off edges to the back edges.
Taking great care, pin the remainder of
the bands in place so that the miters fit
around the corners. Attach with a flat
seam. Attach armbands in same manner.
Attach buttons.

Patchwork Raglan Sweater

Materials
Using heavy weight worsted yarns: 3½oz each of nine colors (A–I, "I" being used for the bands and cuffs); 1oz each of three colors (H,K and L); the roll neck may be worked in the remaining colors – the sample was worked half in F and half in E.

Needles
One pair of No.5 and one pair of No.7 needles.

Gauge
Using No.7 needles and measured over st st, 18 sts = 4in.

The chart opposite shows the pattern for the front of the sweater.

Key to colors :

A = grey tweed
B = turquoise tweed
C = peach tweed
D = heather
E = purple tweed
F = navy tweed
G = mauve tweed
H = mauve
I = medium blue
J = purple chenille
K = natural
L = bright royal

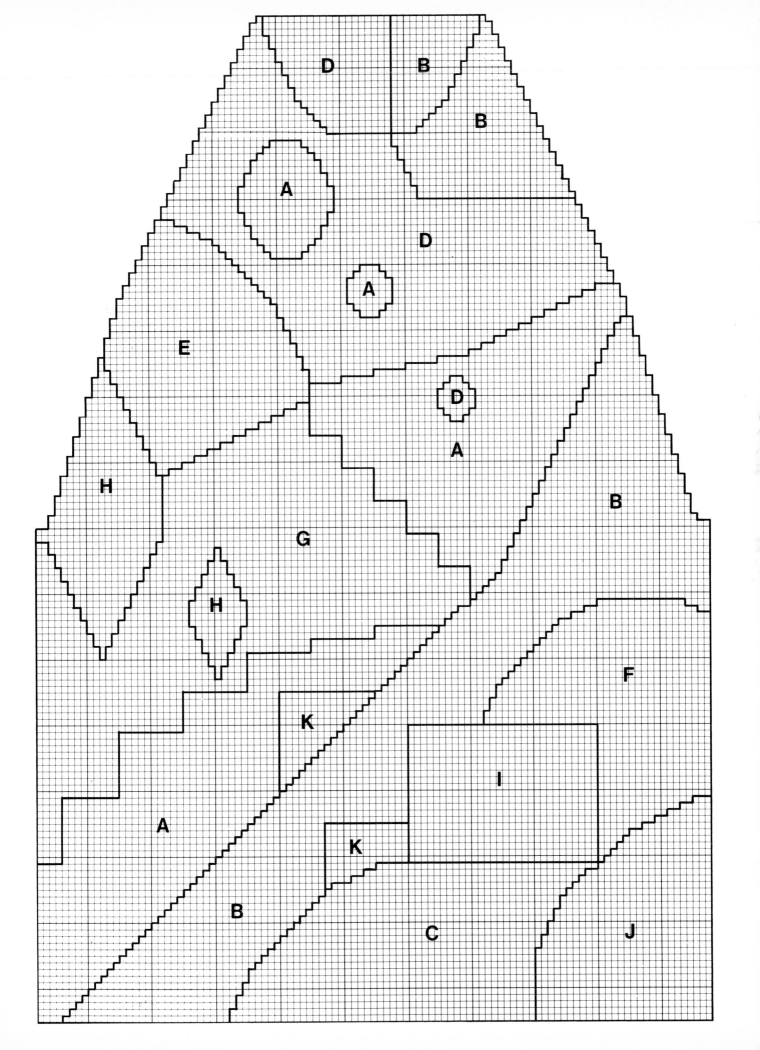

The sample sweater which is illustrated has been worked using both tweed and plain-colored heavy weight worsted yarns, but two ends of light weight worsted yarn may also be used to provide an equivalent weight. If you mix two different colors, a tweed effect will result. The random shapes which are produced by the pattern enable you to change the shapes if you find that your yarn is running out, without affecting the overall design. Written in one size, the sweater is a baggy fit on women and a standard fit on men (extra width and length is added to the cuffs for the man's version).

Back
Using No.5 needles and rib color, cast on 106 sts.
Row 1: *k1, p1, rep from * to end.
Keep repeating this row to form single rib until it measures 2½in. Change to No.7 needles and work from the chart, using a separate ball of yarn for each color area (*see* Techniques, page 10). When the correct point is reached on the chart, **shape armholes** by binding off 2 sts at beg of next 2 rows. Dec 1 st at each end of the next and every following 3rd row until 80 sts remain. Then dec 1 st at each end of

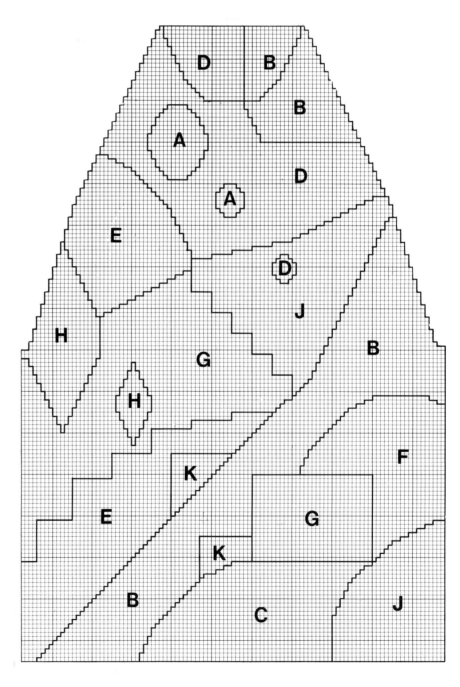

Chart showing the back of the Patchwork Raglan Sweater.

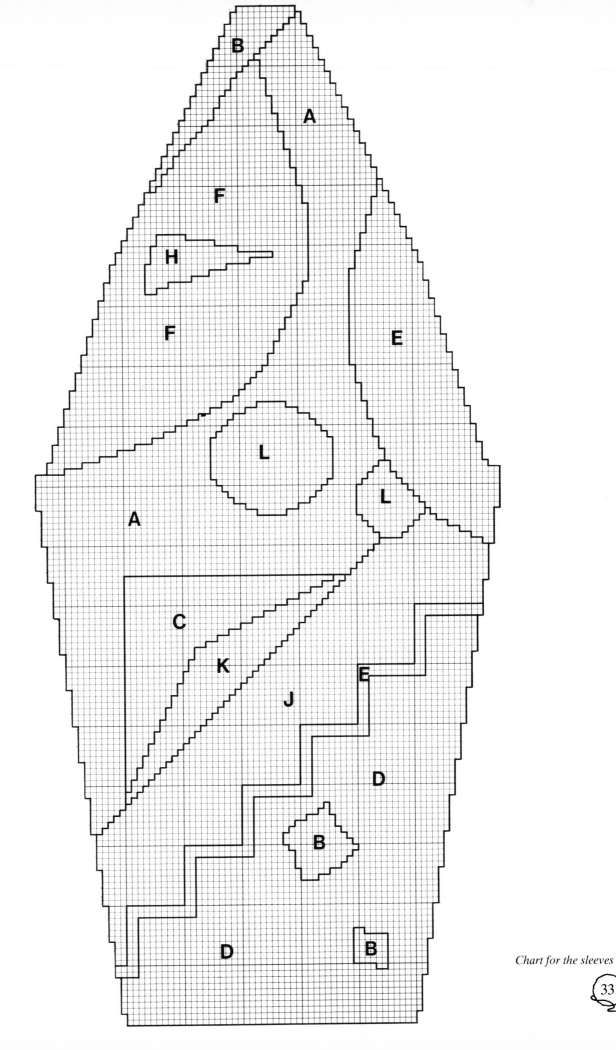

Chart for the sleeves

every alt row until 36 sts remain. Work 1 row, then leave sts on a holder.

Front
Work as for back, but shaping neck where indicated.

Sleeves (Make 2)
Using No.5 needles and rib color, cast on 44/50 sts and work in single rib for 2½/4in. Change to No.7 needles and start working from chart, inc 6/0 sts evenly across the first row. Cont to inc 1 st at each end of the 2nd and every following 6th row until you have 80 sts. Work even to the point on the chart where **raglan shaping** starts: bind off 2 sts at beg of next 2 rows, then dec 1 st at each end of the next and every following 3rd row until you have 52 sts. Then dec 1 st at each end of every alt row until 10 sts remain. Leave these sts on a holder. Both sleeves are worked exactly the same.

Roll neck
Using No.5 needles and a suitable color from your remaining yarns, slip the right sleeve sts on to the needle, followed by the back sts and the left sleeve. Knit up 14 sts down the left side, 14 sts across the front and 14 sts up the other side (98 sts on the needle). Knit the first (WS) row, then work in single rib for 7in, changing color where necessary. Bind off loosely in ribbing.

Finishing
Join the raglans and the rib edges with flat seams. Join the remaining seams with flat seams, taking care to match the color areas on the sleeves and body. **NOTE:** The left and right sleeves can be distinguished by the areas of color, which match those on the body.

Multi-stripe Sweater

This long-line, drop-shoulder sweater uses twelve different colors to create a softly striped pattern. The effect is achieved by using a simple knit and purl stitch to break up the line where the color changes, giving it a more subtle appearance than stripes that are worked in plain stockinette stitch. Changing the colors every two rows helps them to blend together, which means that less attractive colors may be used up because they will be enhanced by the colors used in the rows above and below. The sweater is worked in fingering weight yarn and, being a very loose style, one size fits all.

Pattern
Row 1: *k1, p1, rep from * to end.
Rows 2 and 4: knit.
Row 3: *p1, k1, rep from * to end.

Back
Using No.2 needles and color A, cast on 168 sts.
Row 1: *k1, p1, rep from * to end.
Keep repeating this row to form single rib. After the first row, change to color B and rib 2 rows. Change to color C and rib 2 rows. Change to color D and rib 2 more rows. Return to color A and cont in rib until it measures 2½in from beg, ending with a WS row, having inc 1 st at each end of it. Change to No.4 needles and cont in pattern, changing color every 2 rows. When work measures 28¾in, leave sts on a spare needle.

Front
Work as for back until piece measures 25¼in. **Shape neck**: next row: work pattern over 70 sts, bind off 30 sts, work pattern to end. Cont with this set of sts, leaving others on a holder. Dec 1 st at neck edge on every row until 49 sts remain. Work even until it matches the back. Leave sts on a holder. Return to other side of neck, join yarn in at neck edge and work to match the first side.

Sleeves
Using No.2 needles and color A, cast on 60 sts and work rib in stripe sequence, as for back, ending with a RS row. Purl the next row, inc into every 6th st (70 sts). Change to No.4 needles and cont in pattern, inc 1 st at each end of next and every following 5th row until you have 130 sts. Work even until sleeve measures 17¼in. Bind off loosely.

Neckband
Knit left shoulder seam tog (*see* Techniques, page 15). Slip the 72 back neck sts on to a No.2 needle, then, using color A, knit up 24 sts down the left side of neck, 30 sts across front and 24 sts up other side (150 sts). Purl the first (WS) row. Work in single rib for 4 rows. Change to color B, rib 1 row. Change to color C, rib 1 row. Change to color D, rib 1 row. Cont in color A until rib measures 2½in. Leave sts on a thread.

Finishing
Because this pattern produces so many ends that need securing, it is a good idea to do so by running lines of machine stitching along the edges before you sew up (*see* Techniques, page 17).
Knit the right shoulder seam tog. Join the neckband edges with a flat seam. Turn the rib in on itself and slip st the held sts to the inside of the neck, taking care not to twist it (*see* Techniques, page 14).
Open body out and pin sleeves into position, smoothing them flat and taking care not to bunch them. Join with a narrow backstitch. Join side and sleeve seams with a flat seam over ribs and a narrow backstitch over pattern.

Materials
Fingering weight wool: 1¾oz for each of the 12 stripe colors (A–L), plus an extra 1¾oz for the main color for the ribbing. Because this is a very long sweater, if you find that you have slightly less than the required quantity of each color, you can reduce the body length by a few inches. Knit the sleeves first, however, so that you do not run out of any of the colors while you are working them.

Needles
One pair of No.2 and one pair of No.4 needles.

Gauge
Using No.4 needles and measured over pattern: 28 sts = 4in.

Pastel colorway uses RS of stitch.
Rust colorway uses WS of stitch.

Tweed Effect, Slashed-neck Sweater

Materials

Using various mixtures of wool/cotton/linen/silk, the total weight of the sweater is 21oz. Plus an extra 1¾oz to allow for wastage because yarns may only be joined in at the beginning of rounds or rows.

NOTE: If you are using predominantly synthetic yarns, fewer balls will be required because synthetics, being lighter in weight, go further.

Needles

One pair of No.7 and one pair of No.10 needles. One No.7 circular needle and one No.10 circular needle, both 29in long.

Gauge

Using No.10 needles, doubled yarn and measured over st st; 17 sts = 4in.

The main parts of this intricate-looking sweater are, in fact, worked entirely in stockinette stitch. The color pattern is created simply by using two ends of different colored yarns, the combinations of which are continually changed. Extra texture and color are added by using fancy yarns, which include slubs and bouclés. Both fine and medium weight yarns may be used because mixing the two evens out the overall gauge. Because the yarns are being changed often, it is advisable to leave them attached for a few rows, carry them up the side of the work and then use them again. This minimizes the number of ends that are created which will have to be secured at the finishing stage. The use of a circular needle for the body, up to the beginning of the armholes, reduces the number of ends even further because each yarn is always ready to be used again at the beginning of a round. When you are using straight needles, try to change yarn at the end of an even number of rows so that yarns will not be left at the wrong end of a row when you come to use them again.

The sweater is a one-sized garment of generous proportions with a drop shoulder so that it is suitable for any size or shape.

Back and front

Using a No.7 circular needle and yarns chosen for ribs, cast on 220 sts.
Round 1: *k1, p1, rep from * to end.
Keep repeating this round to form single rib for 1½in. Change to a No.10 circular needle and cont in st st, changing one or both of yarns used when appropriate.
When work measures 16¼in, **divide for armholes**: work across half the sts with No.10 needles. Leave the other half on the circular needle as a holder. Cont with these sts on the pair of No.10 needles. When work measures 24½in, change to No.7 needles and rib yarns and work in single rib for 1¼in. Leave sts on a holder. Return to sts left on circular needle and work to match first side. Now place the front and back tog, RS facing. Knit tog the first 35 sts to form one shoulder seam (*see* Techniques, page 15). Bind off the next 40 sts to form the back neck, knitwise, and knit tog the second shoulder seam. Return to the front neck sts and bind these off knitwise.

Sleeves

Using No.7 needles and rib yarns, cast on 40 sts and work in single rib for 1½in. Change to No.10 needles and cont in st st in color pattern, inc 1 st at each end of next 4 rows. Then inc 1 st at each end of every 4th row until there are 80 sts on the needles. Work even until the sleeve measures 15¾in. Bind off loosely.

Finishing

Join the sleeve seam using a flat seam over the ribs and a narrow backstitch over the st st (securing the ends as you do so, *see* Techniques, page 17). Pin sleeves into armholes, distributing the fabric evenly and join with a narrow backstitch.

Landscape Jacket

A neat, cropped, patchwork jacket which can be made in a combination of many textures and colors. Use chunky weight yarns or simply double or triple any yarns of your choice to ensure the correct gauge.

Pocket lining
Using No.10 needles, cast on 18 sts in main color. Work st st for 15 rows. Leave sts on a spare needle.

Right front
Using No.9 needles and rib color, cast on 35 sts. K1, p1 rib for 4 rows. Change to

The charts on pages 41/43 show the distribution of the different colors and wools in the Landscape Jacket illustrated. For key to the colors see page 43.
The chart below is for the sleeves. The second letter is for the left sleeve.

Key to colors :
A = brown wool
B = cream wool
C = green wool
D = heather wool
E = royal blue wool
F = moss green chenille
G = yellow wool
H = fuchsia angora
I = pink chenille
J = heather fleck wool
K = variegated mauve mohair
L = purple wool
M = red tweed wool
N = black tweed wool
O = turquoise cotton
P = turquoise fleck ribbon

Materials
Assorted yarns equivalent to bulky weight. Total weight of yarn required is 32oz. 5 buttons.

Needles
One pair of No.9 and one pair of No.10 needles.

Gauge
Using No.10 needles and measured over st st, 14 sts and 18 rows = 4in.

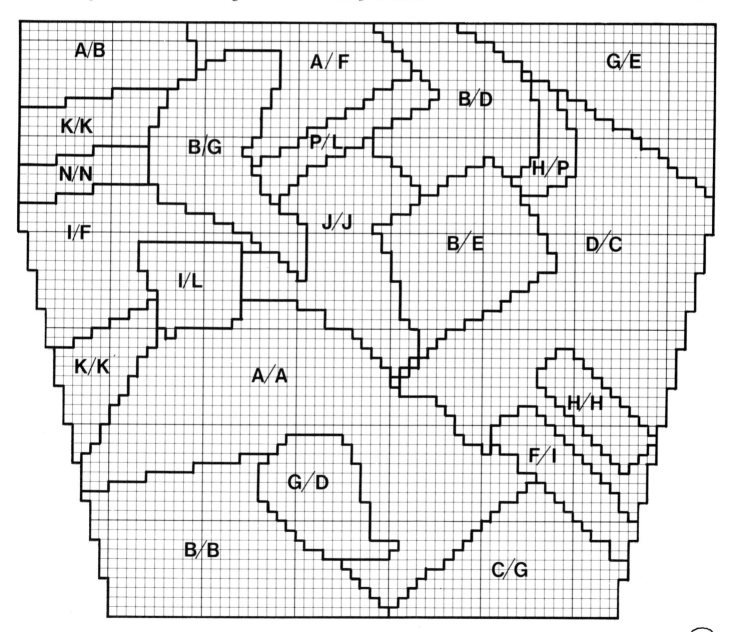

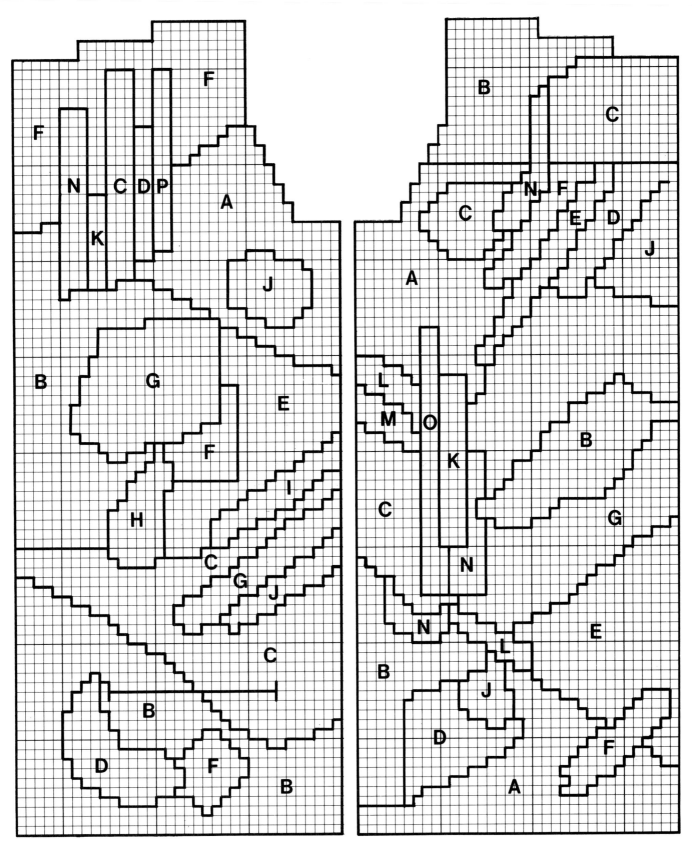

The chart above shows the front of the jacket.

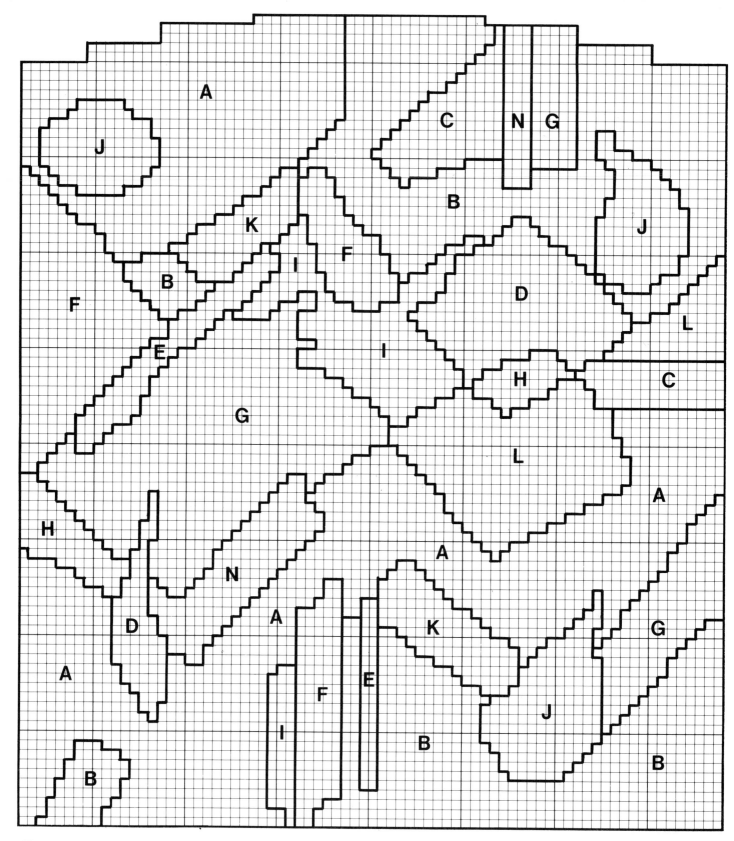

Chart for the back of the jacket.

No.10 needles and, working in st st, follow chart for 14 rows.

Pocket row
Cont to follow the chart, k7, slip 18 sts on to a stitch holder, rejoin yarn, knit to end. Return row: p10, purl across sts held for pocket lining, p to end. Cont following the chart, then begin **neck shaping**: with RS facing, bind off 5 sts at beg of the next row, then bind off 1 st at neck edge on the next 5 alt rows (25 sts). Work even to row 82. Cont to work even at neck edge, **shape shoulder**: row 82: bind off 7 sts at beg of this row, then bind off 8 sts at beg of the next alt row. Work 1 row. Bind off remaining 10 sts.

Left front
Work as for right front, reversing shapings and omitting the pocket.

Back
Using No.9 needles, cast on 75 sts. K1, p1 rib for 5 rows. Change to No.10 needles and begin following the chart in st st to shoulder shaping. Bind off 7 sts at beg of the next 2 rows, bind off 8 sts at beg of the next 2 rows and 10 sts at beg of the following 2 rows. Bind off remaining 25 sts.

Sleeves (Make 2)
Using No.9 needles, cast on 56 sts.
Row 1: k1, p1 to last st, k1.
Row 2: p1, k1 to last st, p1.
Repeat these 2 rows 5 more times.
Change to No.10 needles and, working in

st st, follow the chart, inc 1 st at each end of every 4th row until you have 75 sts. Work even until the chart is complete.

Buttonband
Using No.9 needles, cast on 8 sts. Work in k1, p1 rib until band reaches the beg of the neck shaping when slightly stretched. Leave sts on a safety-pin.

Buttonhole band
Work as for buttonband, making buttonholes as follows, beg on rows 5, 21, 39, 55, 71:
Row 1: rib 3, bind off 2, rib 3.
Row 2: rib 3, bind on 2, rib 3.

Neckband
Join shoulders using a flat seam and stitch front bands in place. Using No.9 needles, pick up 8 sts from buttonhole band, 17 sts up right side, 25 sts across back, 17 sts down left side and 8 sts from buttonband (75 sts).
Row 1: k1, p1 to last st, k1.
Row 2: p1, k1 to last st, p1.
Repeat these 2 rows once more. Bind off.

Pocket trim
Using No.9 needles, pick up 18 sts held for pocket trim. K1, p1 rib for 4 rows, bind off. Stitch pocket lining and sides of trim in place.

Finishing
Join sleeves to body and join seam sleeve and side seams with a flat seam. Sew buttons.

Textured Stitch Sweater

Materials

The total weight required is approx 18oz, which would be plus a small amount to allow for wastage. Because so many very different yarn weights may be used, it is advisable to have a few yarns in reserve and to introduce as many different colors and types of yarn as you feel the design demands. As the neckline is the focal point of the sweater, however, it is a good idea to set aside approx 1¾oz of a yarn you particularly like, rather than having to work the collar in whatever is left over.

Needles

One pair of No.5 and one pair of No.7 needles.

Gauge

Using No.7 needles, the finest yarn you have and measured over st st, 20 sts = 4in.

NOTE: This is a standard gauge for a worsted weight wool or a firmly knitted average mohair. Use this gauge as a guideline through-out. If you find that a particular yarn knits up more bulky than the pattern, use a smaller sized needle when working with it so that the gauge remains uniform.

The grey version shows frequent changes of yarn and stitch.

By the use of a few very basic stitch variations and by choosing different types of yarn, what appears to be an intricately textured pattern may be produced with the minimum amount of effort. The introduction of texture is a good idea when the odd balls with which you are working are either similar in color or are quite dull (see illustration close-ups for the types of yarns that have been used).

Stitches

Garter stitch

Knit every row. Single rows or a number of rows may be used to create ridges, sandwiched with st st to give them definition.

Moss stitch

Row 1: *k1, p1, rep from * to end.
Row 2: *p1, k1, rep from * to end.

Eyelets

Row 1 (WS): knit.
Row 2: k1, *k2 tog, yo, rep from * to last st, k1.
Row 3: knit.

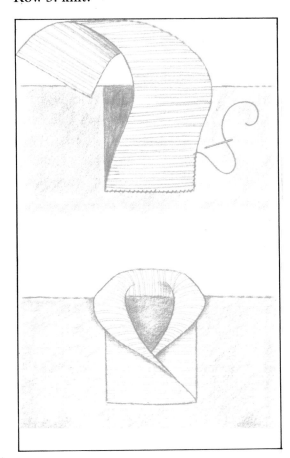

Attaching the collar.

Slip stitch

Row 1 (RS): change to next color. K1, * k1, sl 1 with yarn at back, rep from * to last st, k1.
Row 2: p1, *p1, sl 1 with yarn at front, rep from * to last st, p1.
Row 3: knit (with color in use, previous color or a new color, depending on the color mix which you require).
Use st st and reverse st st in addition and mix the sts up as much as possible to create the maximum number of combinations. Change knit rows to purl and vice versa where desired.

The cream version shows wider bands of yarns and stitches.

Back

Select a smooth yarn of which you have a fair amount to work the ribs. Using this and No.5 needles, cast on 114 sts.

Row 1 (WS): *k1, p1, rep from * to end.
Row 2: *k1 tbl, p1, rep from * to end.
These 2 rows form single twisted rib. Work for 2½in, inc 1 st at either end of the last row. Change to No.7 needles and cont in pattern, changing yarn at random to suit the pattern – i.e., textured or multi-colored yarns for plain sts and plain yarns for textured sts. Make a note of how many rows you have worked in each st so that you will be able to duplicate it on the front and sleeves. A slight variation is acceptable, however, especially if you think that you can improve on what has already been done. Work until it measures 24½in from the beg. Bind off.

Front

Work as for back until piece measures 15¾in. **Shape neck**: work pattern over 43 sts, bind off 30, work pattern over 43 sts. Cont with this set of sts, leaving the others on a holder. When work matches back, bind off. Return to held sts, join yarn in at neck edge and work to match first side. Bind off.

Sleeves

Using No.5 needles and the same color as you have used for the bands (otherwise a complimentary color will be acceptable if you do not have a sufficient quantity), cast on 40 sts and work in single twisted rib for 2½in. Change to No.7 needles and work in pattern, inc 4 sts evenly across the first row. Then dec 1 st at each end of next and every following 4th row until you have 92 sts. Work even until the sleeve measures 17in. Bind off loosely.

Collar

Using No.5 needles and a suitable color for the collar, cast on 153 sts and work in single twisted rib for 6in, working in bands of different yarns if required. Bind off loosely.

Finishing

Join shoulder seams with a flat seam. Open work out so that the sleeves may be laid flat, fully extended, before they are pinned and attached with a narrow backstitch. Slightly stretch the sleeves rather than bunch them into an imaginary armhole. Join the side and sleeve seams with a flat seam over the ribs and a narrow backstitch over the pattern.
Set shawl collar in as shown in the diagram. Attach with a flat seam.

Side-stripe Children's Jacket

A mini "coat of many colors" which is knitted in mohair using only basic garter stitch (knit every row). The yoke and cuffs are cleverly formed by turning the work mid-row, leaving the stitches unworked. The one size fits 5 to 6-year-olds.

Materials

Using mohair with a low synthetic content: 1¾oz each of the eight colors (A-H), plus an extra 1oz of one color for the front bands and collar. This is the minimum required, so it is a good idea to have a slightly larger quantity in 4 of the colors, as these can be used on the rows that form the cuffs.
2 large buttons.

Needles

1 pair of No.8 and one pair of No.9 needles.

Gauge

Using No.9 needles and measured over garter st, 16 sts = 4in.

Back

(Starting at the right side seam.)
Using No.9 needles and color A, cast on 56 sts and knit 4 rows. Change to color B and knit 4 rows. Joining in color C, cast on 23 sts at beg of next row and k to end (79 sts).
Rows 2 and 3: k to last 23 sts, turn and k to end.
Row 4: k to end.
Row 5: change to color D and k to end.
Rows 6 and 7: repeat rows 2 and 3.
Row 8: k to end.
The last 4 rows form the pattern. Keep repeating the pattern, changing color every 4 rows, as established, until all 8 colors have been worked. Keep repeating the color sequence until 45 color stripes have been worked from the armhole cast-on edge. Next row: change color, bind off the first 23 sts and k to end. Knit the next 3 rows, change to color A and knit 4 more rows. Bind off.

Left front

Work as for back, but reverse the color sequence. When 15 color stripes have been worked from the very beginning, **shape neck** (still cont in color sequence throughout): bind off 4 sts at beg of next row and then dec 1 st at neck edge on every row that comes to the neck edge, until 69 sts remain. (**NOTE:** Cont turning work at exactly the same point, although there are fewer sts on the needle.) Now work without decs until 23 color stripes have been worked from the very beg. Change to color chosen for front bands and knit 6 rows. Bind off loosely.

Right front

Using No.9 needles and front band color, cast on 69 sts and knit 2 rows. Next row: **form buttonholes**: *k3, bind off 2, rep from * and then k to end. Knit the next row, casting on 2 sts above those bound off on previous rows. Knit 2 more rows. Now begin color sequence, in reverse order to the left front.
Row 1: k to end.
Rows 2 and 3: k to last 13 sts, turn and k to end.
Row 4: k to end.
Repeat last 4 rows, changing color every 4 rows, until 4 color stripes have been worked. **Shape neck**: inc 1 st at beg of next and every following row that comes to this edge until there are 75 sts on the needle

(turning work at the same point). Cont in pattern, casting on 4 sts at beg of next neck edge row. When 21 color stripes have been worked from the beg, bind off 23 sts at beg of next row. Knit 4 rows in next color without turning. Change color and knit 4 more rows. Bind off.

Sleeves

Using No.9 needles and color A, cast on 20 sts and k 1 row.
Next row: cast on 10 sts, k to end. Change to color B and repeat the last 2 rows. Change to color C, k 1 row. Next row: cast on 8 sts, k to end.
Rows 2 and 3: change to color D, k1, inc 1, k to last 8 sts, turn and k to end.
Row 4: change to color E, k1, inc 1, k to end.
Row 5: k to end.
Keeping in color sequence, keep alternating rows 2 and 3 with rows 4 and 5 until you have 60 sts on the needle. Now work the sleeve head edge straight for 36 rows, but cont to shape the 8 st cuff by turning rows as before. When these 36 rows have been worked, start dec 1 st at this edge on every alt row (still maintaining turned rows), until 48 sts remain on the needle. Cast off 8 sts at beg of next WS row, k to end.
Row 2: k to end.
Row 3: bind off 10 sts, k to end.
Repeat these last 2 rows once more.
Knit 1 row and then bind off the remaining 20 sts (this should complete the 4 color stripes which have not been turned to match the first side).

Collar

Using No.8 needles and color chosen for collar, cast on 76 sts and knit every row until it measures 2in. Bind off.

Finishing

Join shoulder seams with a narrow backstitch, securing the ends as you do so (*see* Techniques, page 17). Join side and sleeve seams with a flat seam. Set the sleeves in with a narrow backstitch, securing the ends as before.
The collar should be attached to the neckline at the bound-off edge with a flat seam. It should reach around the neck but stop short of the front bands so that these may overlap.
Attach buttons.

Shoulder Pads

One of the most professional ways of adding a finishing touch to a knitted jacket or sweater is to make matching shoulder pads. Knitted shoulder pads are nicer than ones made from foam and are a clever way of using up a left-over ball of yarn. The type of pad which this pattern makes is not suitable for raglan shoulders as these require a round shape. Use the yarn doubled, but on the same sized needles as

Materials
Worsted weight yarn:
1oz.

Needles
One pair of No.6 needles.

Gauge
Using No.6 needles, worsted weight yarn and measured over garter st (knit every row), 20 sts = 4in.

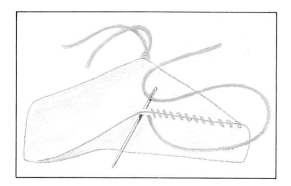

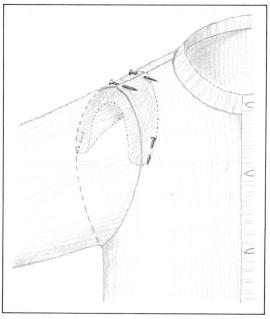

*for the main garment and this will produce
a good, firm pad. The shoulder pads
illustrated here were worked in worsted
weight yarn.*

Using No.6 needles and leaving an end of
yarn for sewing into the garment, cast on
3 sts. Knit every row, inc 1 st each end of
every alt row until you have 33 sts. Now
work even for 1½in before binding off,
leaving a longer end for sewing. Turn the
straight piece back on itself, as shown in
the illustration and slip stitch down.
The most important part of the method is
to attach the pads to the garment so that
they sit correctly and do not pull the fabric
out of shape. Do not turn the garment
inside out, but fold the pad in half and slip
it inside the garment. The fold line should
correspond to the line of the shoulder
seam, with the thick edge along the line of
the armhole seam, as shown. Hold the

garment up so that it takes its own weight,
as it will do when it is worn, and pin the
pad in position through the RS of the
garment as shown. Only when the pad is
firmly in position should the garment be
turned inside out and stitched. The point
of the pad is attached to the shoulder
seam while the 2 ends of the thick edge
are sewn to the armhole seam. Attach the
pads only at these three points; never
attach a pad to the knitted fabric itself as
this will pull the stitches out of shape and
be visible on the RS of the work.

Children's Striped Sweater

A simple, drop-shoulder sweater with shoulder buttoning. The sweater is worked in two sizes, the difference being the weight of the yarn and the size of the needles. By keeping the stripes fairly narrow, it is possible to vary the pattern. You can add extra stripes if you do not have a sufficient quantity of one particular color and substitute colors if you run out unexpectedly (see the yellow stripes at the top of the sweater sleeves, which were introduced when the grey ran out). Use the stripe sequences on the charts as a guideline only. The babies' sweater is worked in fingering weight baby yarn and is suitable for 18-month to 2-year-olds. The toddlers' sweater is worked in light weight worsted yarn and will fit 3 to 4-year-olds. As with most children's garments, synthetic fibers are far more practical from the point of view of washing. The weights quoted are therefore correct for most synthetics, such as nylon or acrylic yarns. If wools are substituted, allow extra yarn.

Back

Using No.2/No.4 needles and rib color, cast on 85 sts and work in k1, p1 rib for 1¼in. Change to No.4/No.6 needles and work stripe pattern in chosen colors, as shown on chart. When work measures 12/14in, **shape neck**: next RS row: k26, bind off 33, k to end. Cont with this set of sts, leaving the others on a holder. Dec 1 st at neck edge on next 2 alt rows. Change to No.2/No.4 needles and color indicated and work remaining 24 sts in k1, p1 rib for 8/6 rows. Change color again, work 4 more rows in rib. Bind off in rib. Return to held sts, shape as for first side of neck, then work even until work measures 13/15in. Bind off.

Front

Work as for back until piece measures 10¾/12¾in, ending with a WS row. **Shape neck**: work 34 sts, bind off 17 sts, work to end. Cont with this set of sts, dec 1 st at neck edge on every row until 24 sts remain. Work even until piece measures

Materials

Babies' sweater in fingering weight: A (green on chart): 2¾oz; B (white on chart): 1¾oz; C (peach on chart): 1oz.
3 tiny pearl buttons.
Toddlers' sweater in light weight worsted : A (grey on chart): 2¾oz; B (blue on chart): 2¾oz; C (white on chart): 1¾oz; D (yellow on chart): 1¾oz.
3 small pearl buttons.

Needles

Babies' sweater: one pair of No.2, one pair of No.3 and one pair of No.4 needles. **Toddlers' sweater**: one pair of No.4 and one pair of No.6 needles.

Gauge

Using No.4 needles, Fingering weight and measured over st st; 28 sts and 36 rows = 4in. Using No.6 needles, light weight worsted and measured over st st, 24 sts and 32 rows = 4in.

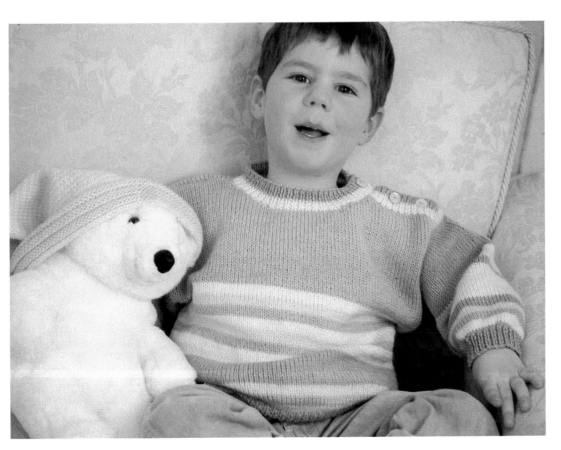

12¼/14¼in from beg. Bind off. Return to the other set of sts and shape to match first side of neck. Work even until piece measures 12½/14½in from beg. Change to No.2/No.4 needles and the color indicated and cont in k1, p1 rib for 8/6 rows. On the next row, change color and **form buttonholes:** *rib 7 sts, bind off 1 st, rep from * once more, rib to end. Rib next row, casting on 1 st above each st bound off on the previous row. Rib 2 more rows. Bind off in ribbing.

Neckband
Join the right shoulder seam with a narrow backstitch. Using a No.2/No.4

The chart shows color stripes as used on toddlers' sample.

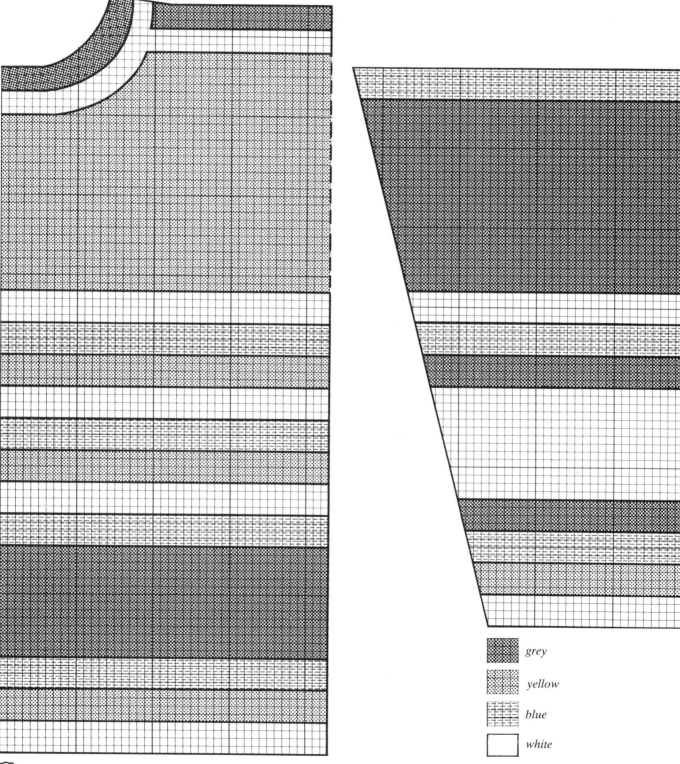

grey

yellow

blue

white

needle and color indicated on chart with RS of work facing you, knit up 20 sts down the left side of the neck (starting at the top edge of buttonhole band), 17 sts across the front, 16 sts up the other side of the neck, then 49 sts across the back neck, finishing at the edge of the buttonband (102 sts). Purl the first row and then rib 6/4 rows. Change color and on the next row form a buttonhole: rib 2, bind off 1 st, rib to end. Rib the next row, casting on a st directly above that bind off on the previous row. Rib 3 more rows. Bind off loosely in ribbing.

Sleeves
Using No.2/No.4 needles and the color indicated, cast on 48 sts and work in k1, p1 rib for 1¼in, ending with a WS row. Next row: knit, inc into every 9th st (53 sts). Change to No.4/No.6 needles and cont in st st, working the stripe pattern as indicated, inc 1 st at each end of every 4th row until you have 87 sts. Work

Chart showing the stripe sequence of the baby's sweater.

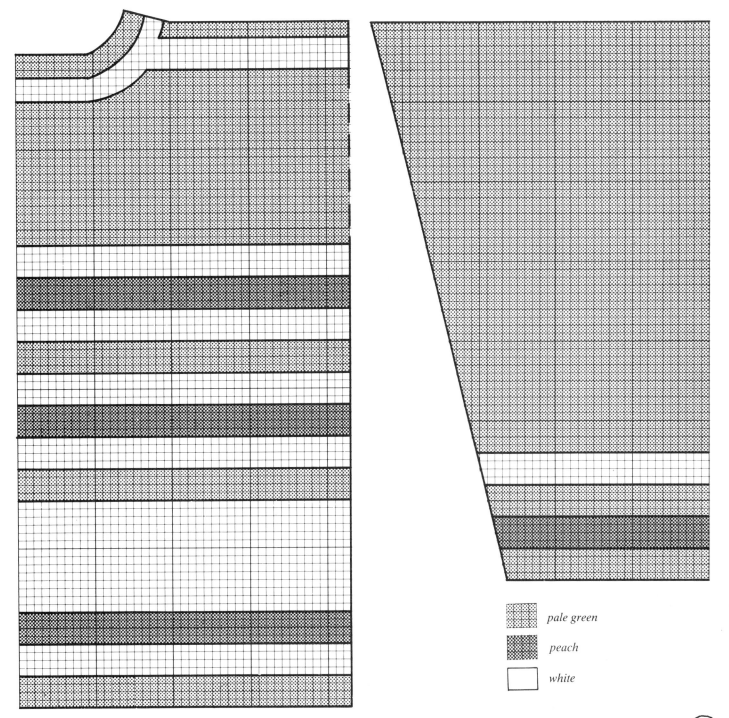

pale green

peach

white

1 row even. Bind off loosely.

Finishing
Open out the body and pin the sleeves, trying not to bunch them. On the buttonband side, overlap the ribs before attaching the sleeve. Stitch with a narrow backstitch. Join side and sleeve seams with a flat seam on the ribs and a narrow backstitch for the st st. Attach buttons to correspond with buttonholes.

Bunny Slippers

A pair of fluffy toddlers' slippers which are worked in mohair with chunky wool soles. The soles are knitted at a very firm gauge to create a durable base. The foot length is 6in.

Materials
Mohair – main color: 1¾oz; **bulky yarn**: 1¾oz.
In addition, a few scraps of pink mohair are needed for the inner ear and nose with a length of finer black yarn for embroidering around the nose and the eyes. One pair of glass eyes.

Needles
One pair of No.6 and one pair of No.7 needles.

Gauge
Using No.6 needles, bulky yarn and measured over st st, 20 sts = 4in. Using No.7 needles, mohair and measured over st st, 18 sts = 4in.

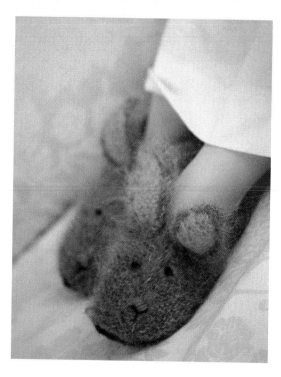

end of every row until there are 62 sts on the needle. Now work even until piece measures 4in from the beg. Bind off.

Ears (Make 2)
Using No.7 needles and main mohair color, cast on 3 sts. Knit 2 rows. Cont knitting every row, inc 1 st at each end of the next and following 6th row (7 sts). Work even for 12 rows. Bind off.

Ear linings (Make 2)
Using No.7 needles and pink mohair, cast on 2 sts. Knit 2 rows. Cont to knit every row, inc into both sts on the next row. Work 12 rows even. Dec 1 st at beg of next 2 rows. K2 tog and pull yarn through to secure, leaving an end for sewing.

Finishing
Join the shaped edges of the uppers to form the center front seam, so that purl side is the right side. Turn inside out and attach to the inside of the sole, working a flat seam around the sole edge.
Slip stitch the ear linings to the ears (the bound-off edge of the ear being its bottom). Position the ears on the fronts of the slippers, slightly gathering the bound-off edge as you slip stitch them to the uppers.
Attach the eyes and embroider the nose using satin st and backstitch (*see* Techniques, page 17), and French knots as shown in the illustration.

Soles (Make 2)
Using No.6 needles and bulky yarn, cast on 4 sts and work in st st, inc 1 st at each end of the 3rd and 5th rows (8 sts). Then inc 1 st at each end of every 4th row until you have 14 sts. Work even until the sole is 5¼in long. Then dec 1 st at each end of every row until 8 sts remain. Bind off.

Uppers
Using No.7 needles and mohair, cast on 30 sts and work in st st, inc 1 st at each

Christmas Pudding Hat

Materials

Pudding: 3oz of heavy weight worsted (if you have approx 1¾oz of the correct color, change to another color when the shaping begins because this part of the hat is hidden by the cream).
Cream: 1oz of light weight worsted. **Holly**: approx ½oz each of dark green and red in any yarn. (The size of the sprig will vary according to the weight of yarn so avoid using anything too thick or too fine.)

Needles

One pair of No.6 and one pair of No.7 needles.

Gauge

Pudding: using No.7 needles and measured over moss st, 18 sts = 4in. **Cream**: using No.6 needles and measured over st st, 22 sts = 4in.

A seasonal head-warmer that is easily worked in basic stitches. The sample has used tweed heavy weight worsted yarn for the pudding and light weight worsted wool for the cream. One size fits all.

Pudding

Using No.7 needles and pudding color, cast on 93 sts.
Row 1: k1, *p1, k1, rep from * to end.
Row 2: *k1, p1, rep from * to last st, k1.
Keep repeating these 2 rows to form moss st. When work measures 6¼in, **shape crown**: on the next row, place a marker in the 11th st and every 18th st after that (5 markers in all). Cont in st st, and on the next row, dec 1 st after each marked st. Cont dec in this manner, on every row, alternating on which side of the marked sts the decs are worked, until 13 sts remain.
Next row: work 2 tog all along row, work last st. Draw the yarn through the remaining sts and secure the end.

Cream

A: Using No.6 needles and cream color, cast on 3 sts. Working in st st, inc 1 st at each end of every row until you have 15 sts, ending with a WS row.
Work 2 more pieces to match.
B: Work as for A, then cont by casting on 3 sts and working to within last 2 sts, inc into next st, k1. Inc 1 st at each end of next row. Repeat last 2 rows.
Next row: cast on 4 sts, work to last 2 sts, inc into next st, k1. Inc 1 st at each end of next row (34 sts).
Work 1 more piece to match.
Now knit across all these pieces, putting them on to the needle in the following order: ABABA (113 sts). Work 2 rows even. On the next row, mark sts as on main hat, but mark them on the 14th, 21st and every following 21st stitch (5 markers in all). Dec as for main hat to end.

Holly sprig

Leaf (make 2): using green and appropriate needles for weight of yarn, cast on 5 sts. Work in st st, *inc 1 st at each end of next 3 rows. Bind off 3 sts at beg of next 2 rows.* Rep from * to * twice more. Dec 1 st at each end of next row. Next row: work 1, work 2 tog. Work remaining 2 sts tog and fasten off.
Berry (make 2): using red and appropriate needles, cast on 2 sts. K1, p1, k1 into both sts (6 sts). Knit 3 rows. Knit 2 tog across next row. K remaining 3 sts tog and fasten off, pulling it into a berry shape.

Finishing

Join the edges of the main hat and the cream with a flat seam. Slip the cream on top of the hat, center the crown and slip st the cream edges through to the wrong side of the main hat. Attach the holly sprig to the top of the crown, stitching through both cream and hat to secure them together.

Bauble Hat

A warm hat which is decorated for the Christmas season. Knitted in mohair, it *uses very small amounts of lurex for the "baubles".*

Materials
Mohair: 1¾oz. 3 lurex colors (thin lurex used triple): 1oz each.

Needles
One pair of No.6 and one pair of No.7 needles.

Gauge
Using No.7 needles and mohair, measured over st st, 18sts = 4in.

Making a pompon

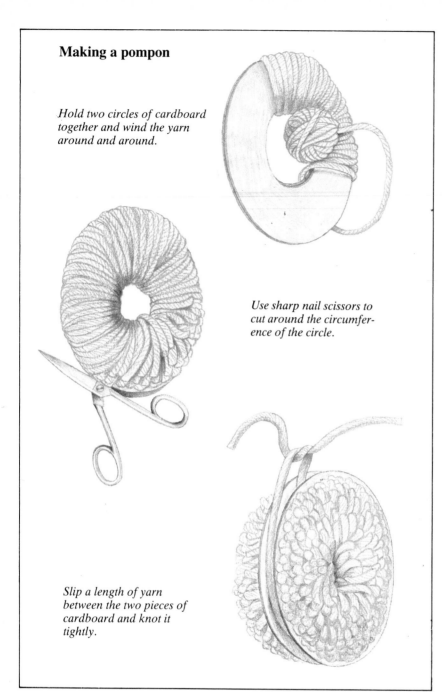

Hold two circles of cardboard together and wind the yarn around and around.

Use sharp nail scissors to cut around the circumference of the circle.

Slip a length of yarn between the two pieces of cardboard and knot it tightly.

Hat

Using mohair and No.6 needles, work as for the Christmas pudding hat (*see* page 59) until the main part measures 1in. Now change to No.7 needles and st st and work from chart. Do not carry any colors at the back of the work. Join extra balls in so that each area of color is separate (*see* Techniques, page 10). When the chart is complete, cont in st st and shape crown as for the Christmas pudding hat.

Finishing

Join edges with a flat seam.

Pompon

Cut out two cardboard circles approx 4in in diameter with holes in the center as shown. Hold the 2 circles together and, using the main color wound into a ball small enough to pass through the center hole, wind the yarn around and around, keeping the strands close together. Cont wrapping the yarn around, working as many layers as you can from the remaining yarn and before the center hole becomes too small for the ball of yarn to pass through.
Using sharp nail scissors, slip a blade between the two layers of cardboard and cut around the circumference of the circle. Slip a length of yarn between the two layers and around the center of what will become the pompon.
Pull tight and knot the yarn before pulling the two pieces of cardboard away (cut them if this proves difficult).
Shake and trim the pompon into shape.

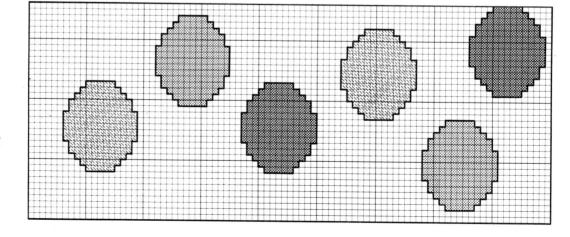

Bauble hat chart The baubles should be knitted as shown.

▨▨▨ light blue

▨▨▨ silver

▨▨▨ dark blue

Pill-box Shaped Hat

A smart little military pill-box shaped hat that is worked on double-pointed needles in light weight worsted yarn. If the same hat is worked in heavy weight or bulky weight yarn, a more substantial, tam-type shape is produced.

Materials
Light weight worsted wool: 1¾oz.

Needles
One set of No.4 and one set of No.6 double-pointed needles.

Gauge
Using No.6 double-pointed needles and measured over st st, 24 sts = 4in.

Crown

Using No.6 double-pointed needles, cast on 8 sts and distribute between the needles to form a round. Knit the first round through the backs of the stitches.
Round 2: inc into every st (16 sts). Knit 1 round.
Round 4: inc into every alt st (24 sts). Knit 2 rounds.
Round 6: Knit 1 round. *k3, inc into next st rep from * to end (30 sts).
Round 8: *k2, inc into next st, rep from * to end (40 sts). Knit 2 rounds.
Round 11: *k3, inc into next st, rep from * to end. Knit 2 rounds.
Continue in pattern as established, working 10 incs on every 3rd round, with an extra st between each inc on each successive inc round, until there are 120 sts on the needles. Bind off very loosely.

Main hat

Using No.4 double-pointed needles, cast on 120 sts and work in alt rounds of knit and purl to produce garter st for ¾in. Change to No.6 double-pointed needles and cont to knit every row to produce st st until the hat is desired depth. Bind off loosely.

Finishing

Press the crown piece flat. Attach the crown to the bound-off edge of the main hat using a flat seam worked on the RS of the work. The combination of the two bound-off edges and the overcast stitches creates the decorative ridge.

Ski Hat

Materials
Worsted weight wool: 1¾oz of each of the two colors.

Needles
One set of double-pointed No.6 needles.

Gauge
Using No.6 needles and measured over st st, 22 sts and 32 rows = 4in.

A stocking cap which is worked in narrow stockinette stitch stripes to keep your head snug when you are on your skiing holiday. The hat can be finished with a pompon or a cord and tassel, as shown. Worked in worsted weight wool, in the round, one size fits all.

Using a set of No.6 needles and color A, cast on 116 sts and knit 6 rounds. *Change to color B and purl 3 rounds. Change to color A and knit 3 rounds.* Rep from * to

* 3 times more. Now cont to knit every round, changing color every round throughout. When work measures 6in divide the sts into 4 groups with a marker before every 29th st. These 4 sts are the axial sts. Dec 1 st on each side of each axial st on the next round (8 sts in all), and every following 8th round until 68 sts remain. Now dec 1 st on each side of each axial st on every 4th round until 12 sts remain. Work 4 more rounds. Next row: k2 tog across row (6 sts). Work 4 more rounds. Thread the yarn through the remaining sts, draw them up and secure them on the inside of the hat.

Finishing
Either make a pompon (*see* page 62) or a tassel and cord (*see* page 83) and attach to the point of the cap.

Yak Herding Hat

A hat with peak and ear flaps, worked in double mohair to keep the wearer warm even on the slopes of the Himalayas. By using different colored mohairs, a two-tone fur effect may be created and accentuated by brushing afterwards.

Main hat

Using No.10½ needles and the two colors chosen for the main part of the hat, cast on 78 sts. Knit every row until work measures 4¾in. **Shape crown**: on the next row, place markers in the 7th st and every 13th st after that (6 markers in all). Now cont in garter st, and on the next row, dec 1 st on either side of each marker st. Work a similar dec row on every 3rd row until 18 sts remain. Next row: k2 tog to end. Draw the yarn through the remaining sts and secure end.

Peak

Using No.10½ needles and peak colors, cast on 28 sts and work in garter st for 2½in. Cont in garter st, dec 1 st at each end of every row until 16 sts remain. Bind off.

Flaps (Make 2)

Using No.10½ needles and same colors as for peak, cast on 15 sts. Work in garter st for 4¾in. Cont in garter st, dec 1 st at each end of next 4 rows (7 sts). Bind off.

Finishing

Attach peak to the front of the hat, by the cast-on edge, using a flat seam. Attach 2 gripper snap fasteners at either end of the peak so that it can be secured to the main hat. Sew the ear flaps on either side of the peak using a flat seam and attaching them to the main hat at the cast-on edge. Stitch ribbons to the tip of each flap so that they may be tied on top of the head when they are not in use.

Brush the hat well with a wire brush to bring up the fluff.

Materials

Yarn with a high-mohair, low-synthetic content: 1¾oz in each of the 2 colors (if you have slightly less, work the peak and flaps in different colors).
(2) 8in lengths of ½in-wide ribbon or tape.
2 gripper snap fasteners.

Needles

One pair of No.10½ needles.

Gauge

Using No.10½ needles and measured over garter st (knit every row), 14 sts = 4in.

Two-tone Gloves

Materials
Fingering weight wool:
just over 1oz for each
color.

Needles
One pair of No.2 and
one pair of No.3
needles.

Gauge
Using No.3 needles and
measured over st st,
30 sts = 4in.

These gloves are worked in fingering weight yarn, using two needles. The back and palm are worked separately, in contrasting colors, so great care should be taken with all the shapings, which should be worked one stitch in from the edge wherever possible to produce the neatest possible edges for the seaming. The one size fits an average-sized woman's hand. The fingers are worked to the desired length.

Left palm
Using No.2 needles and palm color, cast on 28 sts.
Row 1: *k2, p2, rep from * to end.
Keep repeating this row to form double rib for 2in, ending with a WS row. Change to No.3 needles and cont in st st, working 6 rows even. **Shape thumb**:
Next row: k to last 2 sts, inc into next st, k1.
Work 3 rows even.
Next row: k to last 3 sts, inc into next st, k2.
Work 3 rows even.
Cont in pattern as established, inc into the 27th st on next and every 4th row until there are 36 sts. Work 2 rows even. **Work thumb**:
Next row: p9, turn, leaving remaining sts on a holder. Work thumb straight for 2in.
Next row: k2 tog across the row to last st, k1.
Bind off.
With WS facing, join yarn to held sts and work 1½in even, ending with a RS row, inc 1 st at end.
First finger: p7, turn and leave remaining sts on a holder. Work even until piece is ½in short of required length. Dec 1 st at each end of next and 3rd row. Bind off.
Work the rest of the fingers as for the first.

Right palm
Work as for left palm, reversing the position of the thumb and fingers.

Left back
Using No.2 needles and back color, cast on 28 sts and work in double rib for 2in, ending with a WS row. Change to No.3 needles and st st, inc 1 st at beg of first row. Work 3 more rows. **Shape thumb**:
Next row: k1, inc into next st, k to end.
Work 2 rows even.
Next row: p27, inc into next st, p2.

Work 2 rows even.
Next row: k3, inc into next st, k to end.
Cont inc every 3rd row, as established, until there are 37 sts. Work even to the point on the palm where the thumb starts, ending at the thumb edge.
Work thumb: p9, turn and leave remaining sts on a holder. Cast on 2 sts at beg of the next row and then work even for 1½in. Dec 1 st at each end of every row until 3 sts remain. Bind off. With RS facing, knit up 3 sts from the cast-on edge at the base of the thumb and then work across held sts (31 sts), for 1½in, ending at thumb edge.
First finger: k8, turn, leaving remaining sts on a holder. Cast on 2 sts at beg of next row, then work to ½in short of required length. Dec 1 st at each end of every row until 4 sts remain. Bind off.
Second finger: with RS facing, knit up 2 sts from cast-on edge at base of first finger and k the first 9 sts off the holder, leaving the others on it. Cast on 2 sts at beg of next row, then work even until the finger is ½in short of required length. Dec 1 st at each end of every row until 5 sts remain. Bind off.
Third finger: knit up 2 sts from base of 2nd finger and 8 sts from holder. Cast on 2 sts at beg of next row, then work as for first finger.
Fourth finger: knit up 3 sts from base of third finger and then k across remaining held sts. Work even until the finger is ½in short of required length, then shape as for first finger until 3 sts remain. Bind off.

Right back
Work as for left back, reversing the instructions for the thumb and fingers.

Finishing
Join palms to backs with a very neat flat seam, being careful, as you are joining two contrasting colored pieces together.

"Fur" Mittens

Materials
Main color
mohair: 1¾oz; contrast mohair: ½oz; worsted weight wool for palms: 1¾oz.

Needles
One pair of No.4, one pair of No.5 and one pair of No.6 needles.

Gauge
Using No.5 needles, mohair and measured over st st, 20 sts = 4in. Using No.6 needles, worsted weight yarn and measured over st st, 20 sts = 4in.

The mittens are worked in two pieces with worsted weight wool palms and a mohair "fur effect" pattern on the backs. The samples have been worked in a leopard skin-type colorway. The mittens are medium-sized for women.

Backs

Using No.4 needles and main color mohair, cast on 32 sts. Knit 4 rows. Change to No.5 needles and cont in st st (starting with a purl row) working pattern from the chart (using a separate ball of yarn for each color area – i.e., using the intarsia method, *see* Techniques, page 10). Dec 1 st at each end of next and every following alt knit row, while working 2 decs at the center of the knit rows in between, as shown on the chart. When 20 sts remain, change to No.4 needles and work 8 rows in k1, p1 rib. Change to No.5 needles and cont in st st and chart pattern until the top shaping is reached. Dec 1 st at each end of every alt row until 8 sts remain, as shown. Bind off.
When working the second back, reverse the color pattern by working the first row as a knit row.

Left palm piece

Using No.5 needles and palm yarn, cast on 32 sts and knit 4 rows. Change to No.6 needles and work to match front, omitting color pattern, working the rib on No.5 needles. Work to end of ribbing, then change to No.6 needles and work in st st for 3 rows. Next WS row, **shape thumb gusset**: next row: p4, m1 (by working into the st below and then into the st itself), p1, m1, p to end.
Row 2 and all following RS rows: knit.
Row 3: p4, m1, p3, m1, p to end.
Row 5: p4, m1, p5, m1, p to end.
Cont inc 2 sts on either side of gusset on every alt row until there are 34 sts on the needle.
Next RS row: slip the first 16 sts on to a holder and k15, leaving the last 4 sts on a safety-pin. Cont with these 14 sts, working in st st until just short of required thumb length, ending with a WS row.
Next row: k1, *k2 tog, rep from * to end.
Row 2: p2 tog across row.
Draw yarn end through remaining sts and leave tail for sewing.
Return to held sts. Slip the 4 sts on to the needle and then the 16 sts. K across all sts,

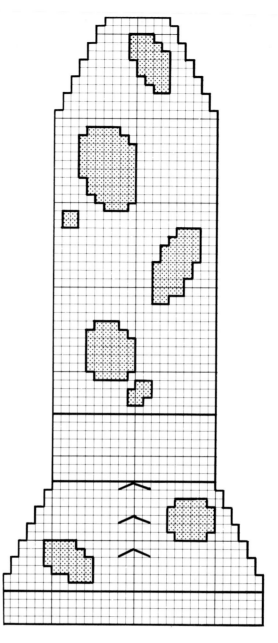

Chart for the back of the mitten. / = k2 tog. \ = sl 1, k1, psso. The dark brown spots are shown by dotted areas.

ensuring that an enlarged strand does not form between the two sets of held sts. Cont in st st to match the front.

Right palm

Work as for left palm, but start the thumb gusset shaping on an RS row so that it comes on the other side of the palm.

Finishing

Join the thumb edges with a flat seam, using the yarn which remains at the tip, having first secured the stitches through which it was drawn. Join the outer edge of the mittens with a flat seam.

Luxury Scarf and Ascot

Materials
**Lacy scarf in fingering
weight silk**: 1¾oz;**ascot
in fingering weight
cashmere**: 1¾oz.

Needles
One pair of No.4
needles.

Gauge
Using No.4 needles and
measured over st st, 28
sts = 4in.

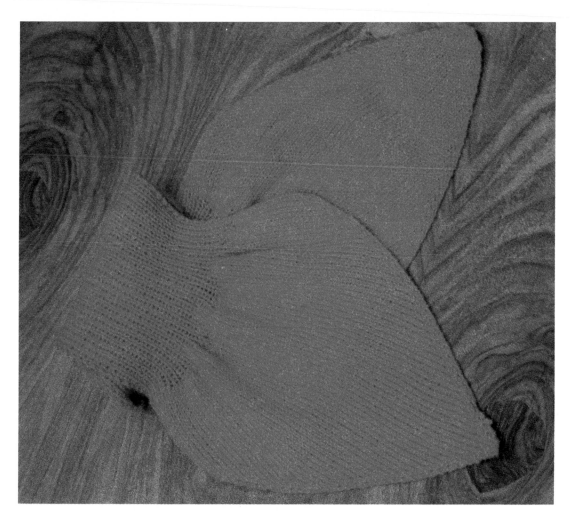

Luxury yarns such as angora, silk, alpaca and cashmere are so expensive that it is a pity to have any left over when a garment is complete. If, however, you are unable to afford the cost of a whole garment made in a luxury yarn, you could treat yourself to an odd ball and make a small item such as a scarf or an ascot.
The lacy scarf is made in silk and the red ascot in cashmere. Each pattern is quoted for fingering weight yarn.

LACY SCARF

Using No.4 needles, cast on 45 sts.
Row 1: k1, *yo, p2 tog, keep rep from *, ending k1.
Repeat this row to form the pattern. Work in pattern until scarf is desired length. Bind off fairly firmly so that the end of the scarf will not flare out.

ASCOT

Using No.4 needles, cast on 3 sts and knit 3 rows, inc 1 st at each end of first and 3rd rows.
Next row: k2, p to last 2 sts, k2.
Row 2: k2, inc 1 (by working into st on row below and then the st itself), k to last 3 sts, inc 1, k2.
Keep repeating these 2 rows until you have 71 sts. Work 14 rows even (maintaining the garter st border).
Next WS row: k2, p6 (p2 tog) 13 times, p3, (p2 tog) 13 times, p6, k2 (45 sts).
Next row: *k1, p1, rep from * to last st, k1.
Row 2: * p1, k1, rep from * to last st, p1.
Keep repeating these 2 rows to form single rib for 15¾in.
Next RS row: k8, inc into next 13 sts, k3, inc into next 13 sts, k8 (71 sts).
Now shape as for other end, working decs instead of incs. When 3 sts remain, bind off.

Diagonal Scarf

This scarf illustrates another way of using up odd balls of yarn. By working the shaping at either end of the row, the stripes are created on the bias and pointed ends are produced which need no finishing. The use of moss stitch throughout prevents the work from curling and breaks up the stripes. The amount of yarn specified makes a scarf approximately 54in long.

Materials
Worsted weight wool: 6oz total weight.
If an equal amount of yarn is available in three colors, two-row stripes are worked from beginning to end, as on the red/grey/beige sample.
If you have twice as much of one color than you have of the other two together, then that color may predominate in a stripe pattern as shown on the green/yellow/tan sample.

Needles
One pair of No.6 needles.

Gauge
Using No.6 needles and measured over moss st, 22 sts = 4in.

Using No.6 needles, cast on 95 sts in your choice of color. **NOTE:** When you have finished using a color, do not break it off if it is to be used again within a few rows, but carry it up the side of the work.
Row 1: *k1, p1, rep from * to last st, k1.
This row forms moss st and is repeated throughout.
Row 2: inc 1, moss st to last 3 sts, work 2 tog, moss st 1.
Row 3: work even in moss st.
Keep repeating these last 2 rows until scarf is desired length (if you are working stripes with a variable depth, finish on the same sequence with which you have started). Bind off.

Argyle Pattern Socks

Possibly the most classic sock design, the pattern is suitable for muted colors as much as for bright ones. These socks will fit any man's shoe size as the foot length is adjustable. Use separate balls of yarn for each individual area of color, carrying only the main color behind the thin stripes. The socks are knitted in fingering weight yarn, a wool mix being recommended for hard wear.

Using No.2 needles and main color, cast on 64 sts.
Row 1: *k1, p1, rep from * to end.
Keep repeating this row to form single rib for 1¼in, ending with a WS row. Change to No.4 needles and cont in st st, working from the chart. When chart is complete, start working on the set of double-pointed needles, in main color only. Put the first and last 16 sts of the row on to the same

Materials
Fingering weight wool/ synthetic mix: **main color**: 1¾oz; **3 contrasting colors**: 1oz each.
NOTE: If you are working a pair of socks for very large feet and you find that you are running short of the main color, work the toe caps in one of the contrast shades.

Needles
One pair of No.2 and one pair of No.4 needles. One set of double-pointed No.4 needles.

Gauge
Using No.4 needles and measured over st st, 28 sts = 4in.

needle and work these 32 sts only for 20 rows, ending with a WS row. **Turn heel:** Next row: k20, sl 1, k1, psso, turn.
Row 2: p9, p2 tog, turn.
Row 3: *k9, sl 1, k1, psso, turn.
Row 4: p9, p2 tog, turn.
Rep from * until 10 sts remain on one needle, ending with a WS row. Knit these 10 sts, then knit up 16 sts along the side of the heel flap. With the 2nd needle, knit across the 32 instep stitches and, with the 3rd needle, knit up 16 sts along the other side of the heel flap, then knit 5 sts from the first needle. Maintain this distribution of sts and knit one round.
Round 2: on first needle, k to last 3 sts, k2 tog, k1. K all sts on 2nd needle. On 3rd needle, k1, sl 1, k1, psso, k to end. Repeat last 2 rounds until 64 sts remain. Cont to work even until foot is 2in short of the required length. **Shape toe:** knit 1 round. Round 2: on first needle, k to last 3 sts, k2 tog, k1. On 2nd needle, k1, sl 1, k1, psso, k to last 3 sts, k2 tog, k1. On 3rd needle, k1, sl 1, k1, psso, k to end. Repeat last 2 rounds until 24 sts remain. Bind off.

Finishing
Join back leg seam and toe tips with a very neat flat seam as the socks will be uncomfortable to wear if the seams are bulky.

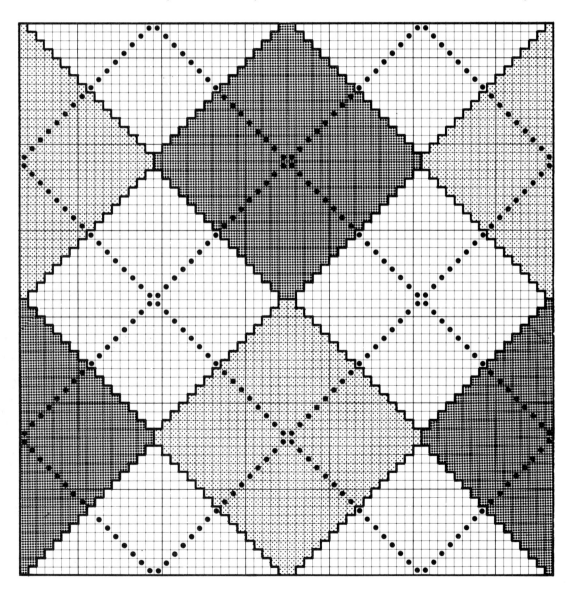

Chart for the Argyle pattern. The plain squares are in a neutral color.

 green

 brown fleck

• yellow

Slip-stitch Pattern Socks

Materials
Using a fingering weight wool/synthetic mix: 1¾oz in each of the two colors.

NOTE: If you are working a pair of socks for very large feet and you find that you are running short of the main color, work the toe caps in the contrasting color.

Needles
One pair of No.2 and one pair of No.4 double-pointed needles. One pair of No.4 single-pointed needles.

Gauge
Using No.4 needles and measured over pattern (cast on 24 sts to work gauge sample), 15 sts = 2in.

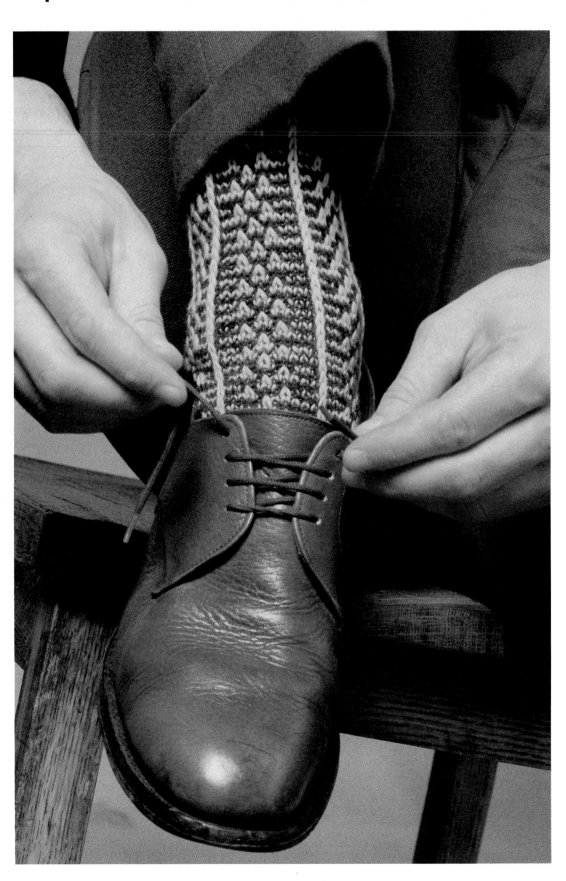

This sock pattern is worked in the opposite manner to the argyle pattern on page 74 because the leg part is worked in the round and the stitches are then divided into two sections for the foot part, as the pattern is continued on the instep, while the heel and sole are worked in main color. The foot size is adjustable and the yarn used is a fingering weight wool mix.

Using a set of No.2 double-pointed needles and main color, cast on 64 sts. Work in rounds of single rib for ¾in. Knit the next round, inc into every 8th st (72 sts). Change to No.4 double-pointed needles and start pattern.
Round 1: in contrasting color, knit.
Round 2: in main color, *sl 1, k3, rep from * to end.
Repeat 2nd and then first rounds.
Round 5: in main color, *sl 1, k5, rep from * to end.
Round 6: repeat round 5.
These 6 rounds form the pattern. Keep repeating until work measures approx 8in, ending with a complete pattern. **Divide for heel**: put the first and last 18 sts of the round on to a No.4 single-pointed needle, leaving remaining sts on a holder. Cont with these sts in main color only, working in st st for 20 rows, ending with a WS row.
Turn heel:
Next row: k22, sl 1, k1, psso, turn.
Row 2: p9, p2 tog, turn.
Row 3: *k9, sl 1, k1, psso turn.
Row 4: p9, p2 tog, turn..
Rep from * until 14 sts remain on one needle, ending with a WS row. Knit up 16 sts along the side of the heel flap, knit across 14 sts of heel and then knit up 16 sts along other side of heel flap (46 sts).
Shape instep:
Next row: purl.
Row 2: k1, sl 1, k1, psso, k to last 3 sts, k2 tog, k1.
Keep repeating last 2 rows until 34 sts remain. Work even until foot is 2in short of desired length. Leave sts on a safety-pin and return to instep sts. Work these sts, in pattern, on a pair of No.4 needles,

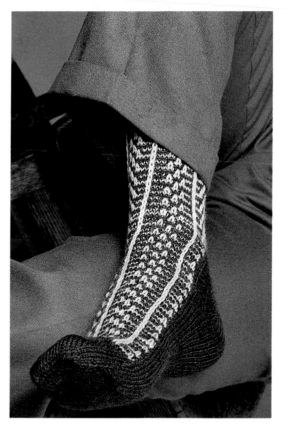

remembering that every alt row the "knit" sts are worked as "purl" sts since the work is no longer in the round. Work until the instep is as long as the sole, ending with a WS row, dec 1 st at each end. **Work toe cap**: cont in main color only, working all the sts in the round, with No.4 double-pointed needles. Place half the sole sts on the first needle, the 34 instep sts on the 2nd needle and the remaining 17 heel sts on the third needle. Knit 1 round.
Round 2: on first needle, k to last 3 sts, k2 tog, k1. On 2nd needle, k1, sl 1, k1, psso, k to last 3 sts, k2 tog, k1. On 3rd needle, k1, sl 1, k1, psso, k to end.
Repeat last 2 rounds until 28 sts remain. Bind off.

Finishing
Join the toe tips and the insteps to the soles using a very neat flat seam as the socks will be uncomfortable to wear if the seams are bulky.

Entrelac Cushion-cover

Materials
A combination of mohairs and heavy worsted weight yarns: a total of 14oz is required for each cushion-cover (each entrelac piece uses approx ¼oz of yarn). one 13¾ × 13¾in pillow form.
1 zipper, if desired.

Needles
One pair No.10½ needles.

Gauge
Using No.10½ needles and measured over st st, 12 sts = 4in.

This pattern uses the same method of knitting as for the mohair jacket on page 18 to create a "quilted" effect cushion-cover. The yarns used are bulky or heavy. The samples have been worked in worsted weight tweed yarn doubled up and heavy worsted weight with one strand of solid combined mohair to give it a tweed effect and a more interesting texture. This is one of the rare occasions when it does not matter whether all the yarns used are the same weight because any variation adds to the quilted effect.

Using No.10½ needles and desired color, cast on 32 sts. Each individual triangle or rectangle is now worked at random in a separate color. Referring to the jacket pattern on page 18, form 4 base triangles and then work from * to * 3 times in all. Finish off with a line of triangles as for jacket back.

Work a second piece to match, although the colors may vary, depending on what yarn you have left.

Finishing
With RS tog, join three sides with a flat seam. Turn the cover right side out, slip the cushion inside and overcast stitch the fourth side or stitch in the zipper if desired, so cushion may be removed when the cover needs to be cleaned.

Circular Cushion-cover

This fan-effect cushion-cover is worked by turning rows so that a circular shape is created. The sample has been worked to give a 3¾in diameter, using eight colors of light weight worsted yarn. More colors may be used to create a rainbow effect. Before you start the pattern, see Techniques, page 9 for the best method of turning.

Using No.6 needles and color A, cast on 40 sts.
Rows 1 and 2: *k to last 4 sts, turn and p to end.
Rows 3 and 4: k to last 8 sts, turn and p to end.
Cont in pattern as established, leaving another 4 sts unworked on every RS row until only 4 sts have been purled.
Next 2 rows: k across all sts and then p across all sts.*

Change to color B and rep from * to *. Keep changing colors until each has been worked, then repeat them once more (16 segments in all). Bind off. Work another circle to match.

Finishing

Join cast-on and bound-off edges with a flat seam. Run a thread around the center circle to pull it in and secure end. With RS tog, join the outer edges of the circles with a flat seam, leaving enough open to allow the cushion to be slipped in. When this has been done, either overcast stitch the opening together or stitch a small zipper in position so that the cushion may be removed when the cover needs to be cleaned.
Make a tassel (*see* page 83) and attach to the center.

Materials
Light weight worsted wool: each segment requires ¼oz of yarn and there are 16 segments on each side of the cover. Allow another ½oz for the tassel. Total: 8oz. The sample illustrated here uses 8 colors (A-H). A small zipper, if desired.

Needles
One pair of No.6 needles.

Gauge
Using No.6 needles and measured over st st, 24 sts = 4in.

Tapestry Cushion-covers

Materials
Main color: 1¾oz light weight worsted wool.
Back: 3½oz light weight worsted wool (this may be worked in stripes using all the left-overs if you don't have 3½oz of one color).
Contrasting colors: a maximum of 1oz light weight worsted wool per

shade. A 13¾ × 13¾in pillow form. Zippers, if desired.

Needles
One pair of No.6 needles.

Gauge
Using No.6 needles and measured over st st, worked in color pattern, 24 sts = 4in.

These cushion-covers, based on old sampler designs, are worked using light weight worsted wool. You can use either faded petit point or rich tapestry colors. Where large areas of color are worked, separate balls of yarn should be used – i.e., using the intarsia method of knitting (see Techniques, page 10). Where separate balls would be impractical, such as the small areas of green leaf on the wreath, carry the yarn which is not in use at the back of the

The chart below is for the pot of flowers design on the cushion.

work – i.e., use the fairisle method of knitting (see Techniques, page 11).

Fronts
(Worked in st st throughout.)
Using No.6 needles and main color, cast on 85 sts.
Pot of flowers: work 4 rows in main color, then begin working from the chart. When the chart is complete, work 4 more rows in main color before binding off.
Wreath: work 12 rows in main color before starting chart. When chart is complete, work 12 more rows in main color before binding off.

Backs
Using the color chosen for the back and No.6 needles, cast on 81 sts and work in st st until it is as long as the front.

Finishing
With RS facing, join three sides of the cushion-cover with a flat seam. Turn the cover right side out, slip cushion in and

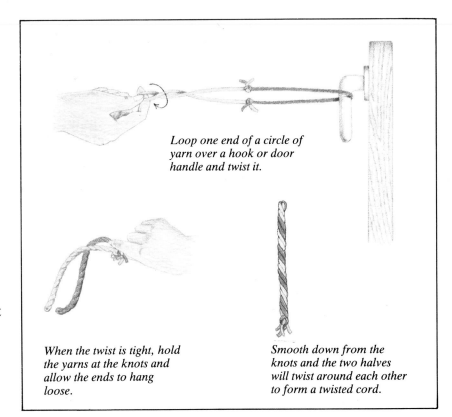

Loop one end of a circle of yarn over a hook or door handle and twist it.

When the twist is tight, hold the yarns at the knots and allow the ends to hang loose.

Smooth down from the knots and the two halves will twist around each other to form a twisted cord.

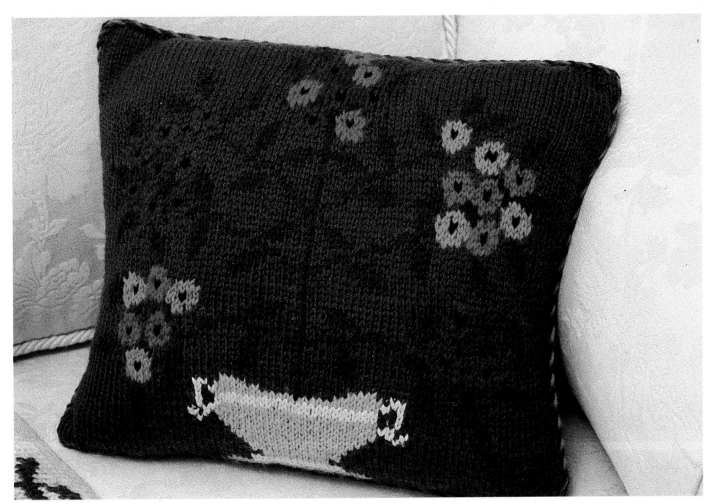

Chart for the floral wreath design.
The background in the center of the design is in a different color from the main background.

overcast stitch the fourth side or stitch in the zipper, if desired.

If braid and tassels are required, they may be worked as follows:

Twisted cord: To make the cord in two colors, cut a piece of yarn in each color, just over twice the required length. Knot them tog to make a continuous circle, as shown, with the knots in the center. Loop one end of the circle over a hook or door handle and keep twisting the yarns with the fingers at one end, holding them taut as you do so. When the twist is tight and will twist up on itself when the yarns are relaxed, take hold of them at the knot point and let the ends hang loose. Smooth down from knots to loop ends and each half should automatically twist around the other, forming the cord. If it looks loose, simply pull the yarns apart and twist them more tightly before folding in half again. Pin the cord around the outer edge of the cushion and slip st into position from the wrong side.

Tassels: wrap the yarn around a piece of cardboard which is slightly longer than the required finished length of the tassel (those in the photograph were made on a piece of cardboard ¾in deep). When it is thick enough, knot a piece of the same color around the strands at the top of the cardboard, then cut along the bottom, as shown. Now wrap another length of yarn around the strands a few inches down from the securing knot at the top. Make sure that this is done tightly, then fasten off. Attach the tassels by the ends of yarn at the top, one in each corner of the cushion.

Tassel

Wrap the yarn around a piece of cardboard that is slightly longer than the length required for the finished tassel.

Tie the strands together at the top and cut them along the bottom.

Wrap a length of yarn tightly around the strands and then fasten off securely.

Lace Table-mats

Materials
Fingering weight
mercerized cotton: 1oz
per mat.

Needles
One set of 5 double-
pointed No.4 needles.

Gauge
Using No.4 double-
pointed needles and
measured over st st,
30 sts = 4in.

*These delicate little mats are worked in
fingering weight cotton, the samples having
used a mercerized variety which has a
sheen. If you have sufficient yarn, the
whole set may be worked in one color,
otherwise it looks perfectly acceptable to
have pairs in compatible colors. They are
worked as medallions – i.e., on double-
pointed needles, knitted from the center
outwards.*

Cast on 8 sts and distribute them between
four of the needles to form a round.
Round 1: (yo, k1) 8 times.
Round 2: k.
Round 3: (yo, k3, yo, kb1) 4 times.
Round 4: k.
Round 5: (yo, k5, yo, kb1) 4 times.
Round 6: k.
Round 7: (yo, k7, yo, kb1) 4 times.
Round 8: k.
Round 9: (yo, sl 1, k1, psso, k2 tog, yo,
k1) 8 times.
Round 10: k.
Round 11: (k1, yo, k2 tog, yo, k2) 8
times.
Round 12: k.
Round 13: (k2, yo, kb1, yo, k3) 8 times.
Round 14: k.
Round 15: (k3, yo, kb1, yo, k4) 8 times.
Round 16: k.
Round 17: (k4, yo, kb1, yo, k5) 8 times.
Round 18: k.
Round 19: (k5, yo, kb1, yo, k6) 8 times.

Round 20: k.
Round 21: (k6, yo, kb1, yo, k7) 8 times.
Round 22: k.
Round 23: (k7, yo, kb1, yo, k8) 8 times.
Round 24: k.
Round 25: (sl 1, k1, psso, k5, yo, k3, yo,
k5, k2 tog, p1) 8 times.
Round 26: (k17, p1) 8 times.
Round 27: (sl 1, k1, psso, k4, yo, k5, yo,
k4, k2 tog, p1) 8 times.
Round 28: as round 26.
Round 29: (sl 1, k1, psso, k3, yo, k1, yo,
sl 1, k1, psso, k1, k2 tog, yo, k1, yo, k3,
k2 tog, p1) 8 times.
Round 30: as round 26.
Round 31: (sl 1, k1, psso, k2, yo, k3, yo,
sl 1, k2 tog, psso, yo, k3, yo, k2, k2 tog,
p1) 8 times.
Round 32: as round 26.
Round 33: (sl 1, k1, psso, yo, k11, yo, k1,
k2 tog, p1) 8 times.
Round 34: as round 26.
Round 35: (sl 1, k1, psso, yo, k1, yo, sl 1,
k1, psso, k1, k2 tog, yo, k1, yo, sl 1, k1,
psso, k1, k2 tog, yo, k1, yo, k2 tog, p1) 8
times.
Round 36: as round 26.
Round 37: sl 1 (yo, k3, yo, sl 1, k2 tog,
psso, yo, k3, yo, sl 1, k2 tog, psso, yo, k3,
yo, k2 tog, sl the next st over this dec) 8
times, pass the first slipped st of the round
over the last decrease.
Round 38: k.
Round 39: (yo, sl 1, k1, psso, k1, k2 tog,
yo, k1, yo, sl 1, k1, psso, k1, k2 tog, yo,
k1, yo, sl 1, k1, psso, k1, k2 tog, yo, k1) 8
times.
Round 40: k.
Round 41: (k1, yo, sl 1, k2 tog, psso, yo,
k3, yo, sl 1, k2 tog, psso, yo, k3, yo, sl 1,
k2 tog, psso, yo, k2) 8 times.
Round 42: purl.
Bind off using a needle at least two sizes
larger so that the bound-off edge will not
curl.

Finishing
Close up center hole when securing the
bound-on end. Steam press with some
spray starch.

Lace Edging

By working a short length of lace in mercerized cotton, plain pillowcases, guest towels, tray-cloths and so on can be given a Victorian feel. The instructions given are for a piece 19¾in long which will fit a standard pillowcase, but the pattern may simply be repeated until it is the required length, each pattern repeat measuring approximately 3¼in.

Edging

Using No.4 needles, cast on 25 sts.
Row 1: yo, k2 tog, yo, k1, (yo, sl 1, k1, psso) twice, yo, k9, (yo, k2 tog) 3 times, k3.
Row 2: sl 1, k2, p24.
Row 3: yo, k2 tog, yo, k3, (yo, sl 1, k1, psso) 3 times, k5, (k2 tog, yo) 4 times, k3.
Row 4: sl 1, k2, p25.
Row 5: (yo, k2 tog) twice, yo, k1, (yo, sl 1, k1, psso) 4 times, k3 (k2 tog, yo) 4 times, k4.
Row 6: sl 1, k2, p26.
Row 7: (yo, k2 tog) twice, yo, k3, (yo, sl 1, k1, psso) 4 times, k1 (k2 tog, yo) 4 times, k1, yo, sl 1, k1, psso, k2.
Row 8: sl 1, k2, p27.
Row 9: (yo, k2 tog) twice, yo, k5, (yo, sl 1, k1, psso) 3 times, yo, sl 1, k2 tog, psso, (yo, k2 tog) twice, yo, k1, (yo, k2 tog) twice, k3.
Row 10: sl 1, k2, p28.
Row 11: (yo, k2 tog) twice, yo, k7 (yo, sl 1, k1, psso) 3 times, k1 (k2 tog, yo) 3 times, k1, (yo, sl 1, k1, psso) twice, k2.
Row 12: sl 1, k2, p29.
Row 13: (yo, k2 tog) twice, yo, k9, (yo, sl 1, k1, psso) twice, yo, sl 1, k2 tog, psso, (yo, k2 tog) twice, yo, k1, (yo, sl 1, k1, psso) twice, k3.
Row 14: sl 1, k2, p30.
Row 15: yo, sl 1, k2 tog, psso, (yo, sl 1, k1, psso) twice, k8, (yo, sl 1, k1, psso) twice, k1, (k2, tog, yo) twice, k1, (yo, sl 1,

Materials

Fingering weight mercerized cotton: 1oz.

Needles

One pair of No.4 needles.

Gauge

Using No.4 needles and measured over st st, 30 sts = 4in.

NOTE: yo in this pattern means place the yarn to the front of the work and then back over the RH needle before placing it into the first st.

k1, psso) 3 times, k2.
Row 16: as row 12.
Row 17: yo, sl 1, k2 tog, psso, (yo, sl 1, k1, psso) twice, k8, yo, sl 1, k1, psso, yo, sl 1, k2 tog, psso, yo, k2 tog, yo, k1, (yo, sl 1, k1, psso) 3 times, k3.
Row 18: as row 10.
Row 19: yo, sl 1, k2 tog, psso, (yo, sl 1, k1, psso) twice, k8, yo, sl 1, k1, psso, k1, k2 tog, yo, k1, (yo, sl 1, k1, psso) 4 times, k2.
Row 20: as row 8.
Row 21: yo, sl 1, k2 tog, psso, (yo, sl 1, k1, psso) twice, k8, yo, sl 1, k2 tog, psso, yo, k1, (yo, sl 1, k1, psso) 4 times, k3.
Row 22: as row 6.
Row 23: (yo, k2 tog) twice, yo, k8, k2 tog, yo, k3, yo, sl 1, k2 tog, psso, (yo, k2 tog) 3 times, yo, k3.
Row 24: as row 8.
Row 25: (yo, k2 tog) twice, yo, k8, (k2 tog, yo) twice, k1, yo, sl 1, k1, psso, yo, sl 1, k2 tog, psso, (yo, k2 tog) twice, yo, k4.
Row 26: as row 10.
Row 27: (yo, k2 tog) twice, yo, k8, (k2 tog, yo) twice, k3, yo, sl 1, k1, psso, yo, sl 1, k2 tog, psso (yo, k2 tog) twice, yo, k3.
Row 28: as row 12.
Row 29: (yo, k2 tog) twice, yo, k8, (k2 tog, yo) 3 times, k1, (yo, sl 1, k1, psso) twice, yo, sl 1, k2 tog, psso, yo) k2 tog, yo, k4.
Row 30: as row 14.
Row 31: yo, sl 1, k2 tog, psso, (yo, sl 1, k1, psso) twice, k5, (k2 tog, yo) 3 times, k3, (yo, sl 1, k1, psso) twice, yo, sl 1, k2

tog, psso, yo, k2 tog, yo, k3.
Row 32: as row 12.
Row 33: yo, sl 1, k2 tog, psso, (yo, sl 1, k1, psso) twice, k3, (k2 tog, yo) 4 times, k1, (yo, sl 1, k1, psso) 3 times, yo, sl 1, k2 tog, psso, yo, k4.
Row 34: as row 10.
Row 35: yo, sl 1, k2 tog, psso, (yo, sl 1, k1, psso) twice, k1, (k2 tog, yo) 4 times, k3, (yo, sl 1, k1, psso) 3 times, yo, sl 1, k2 tog, psso, yo, k3.
Row 36: as row 8.
Row 37: yo, sl 1, k2 tog, psso, yo, sl 1, k1, psso, yo, sl 1, k2 tog, psso, (yo, k2 tog) 3 times, yo, k5, (yo, sl 1, k1, psso) 4 times, k3.
Row 38: as row 6.
Row 39: yo, sl 1, k2 tog, psso, yo, sl 1, k1, psso, k1, (k2 tog, yo) 3 times, k7, (yo, sl 1, k1, psso) 4 times, k2.
Row 40: as row 4.
Row 41: (yo, sl 1, k2 tog, psso) twice, (over, sl 1, k1, psso) twice, yo, k9, (yo, k2 tog) 3 times, k3.
Rows 2-41 inclusive form the pattern (428 rows). Repeat the pattern 5 times more. Bind off.

Finishing
Before you attach the edging to any items, it is advisable to wash, press and starch it into shape and size. The edging may then be applied by hand stitching or, more conveniently, attached with a line of machine stitching along the straight edge.

Loop-stitch Mat

This little bath or bedside mat is extremely quick and easy to make and will use up virtually any odd balls. The sample has used predominantly textured cottons, such as bouclé, slub and fancy synthetic yarns, as can be seen from the detail. These yarns vary in thickness, but are more or less worsted weight. Two different yarns have been worked together all through the pattern to give a more subtle look, but if you are using very bulky yarns, you should use them singly. Since the loop stitch can be difficult to work into a tight stitch, a larger needle is used for each knit row in between. The finished measurement is approximately 26 × 17¼in.

Using No.11 needles, cast on 72 sts as loosely as possible. Knit the first, RS row. Using a No.10½ needle, work the next row as a loop row: **NOTE:** These instructions apply to yarn that is used singly. If you are using doubled yarn, you will have two strands for each one that is illustrated. Place needle into first st, as for a normal knit st.
Bring your left index finger up behind the left needle and, instead of simply winding the yarn around the needle as for a normal st, wind it around the needle and your finger, 3 times as illustrated.
Now pull all 3 strands through the stitch and slip them back on the left-hand needle.
Knit all 4 strands (the 3 new ones plus the original st), as one stitch, through the backs of the loops. When completed, slip your finger into the loop and pull so that each strand is the same length. You should not pull too hard as this will make the stitch on the needle too tight.
Work every stitch in this manner, across the row.
Next row: using a No.11 needle, knit. These 2 rows form the pattern. Keep repeating pattern, changing one or both colors as often as desired (*see* Techniques, page 10). When the mat is large enough, finish with a knit row and then bind off loosely using a No.11 needle.

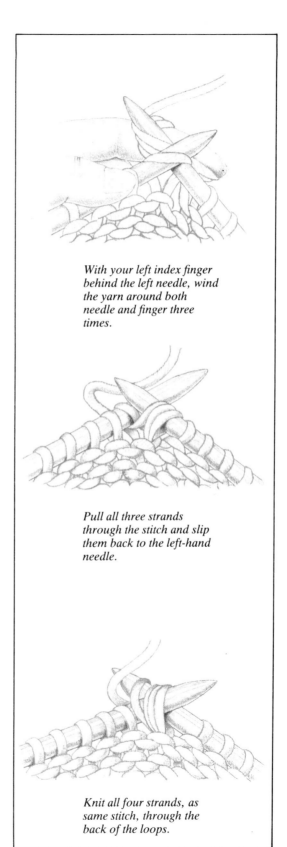

With your left index finger behind the left needle, wind the yarn around both needle and finger three times.

Pull all three strands through the stitch and slip them back to the left-hand needle.

Knit all four strands, as same stitch, through the back of the loops.

Materials
Using predominantly heavy yarns such as cotton mixes, the total weight is approx 25oz. Part-balls may be used, but you should avoid using very small scraps as each loop row takes considerably more yarn than would be used for a normal knit row.

Needles
One No.10½ needle and one pair of No.11 needles.

Gauge
Using the two different size needles, worsted weight type yarns and measured over loop stitch pattern (measure on the WS as the sts are not discernible on the RS): 22 sts = 4in.

Hangers

Materials
Wool, synthetic or cotton-type yarn: 3½oz per cover. A wooden hanger and batting as a base. A small length of ribbon as trim.

Needles
One pair of No.7 needles.

Gauge
Using No.7 needles and measured over st st, 22 sts = 4in.

Padded hangers are essential for fine fabrics and knitwear which tend to become misshapen and unnecessarily creased on normal hangers. Hanger covers may be knitted easily from odd balls using a cheap wooden hanger and a little batting as a base. The pattern is for worsted weight yarns – those that have been used for the samples are rayon ribbon and a silky finished cotton.

Using No.7 needles, cast on 91 sts.
Row 1: *k1, (k2 tog tb1) 3 times, (yo, k1) 5 times, yo, (k2 tog) 3 times, rep from * to last st, k1.
Row 2: purl.
Row 3: knit.
Row 4: purl.
These 4 rows form the pattern. Repeat twice more. Now cont in st st for 4¾in. Bind off loosely.

Finishing
Wrap a 16½in wooden hanger with either a piece of batting, foam, knitted scraps or other available padding type material. Fold the st st part of the cover in half and slip the hook of the hanger through the knitting at the center, on the fold line. Slip stitch around the edges so that the lace part falls as an edging at the bottom of the hanger. Finish with a small ribbon bow at the base of the hook.

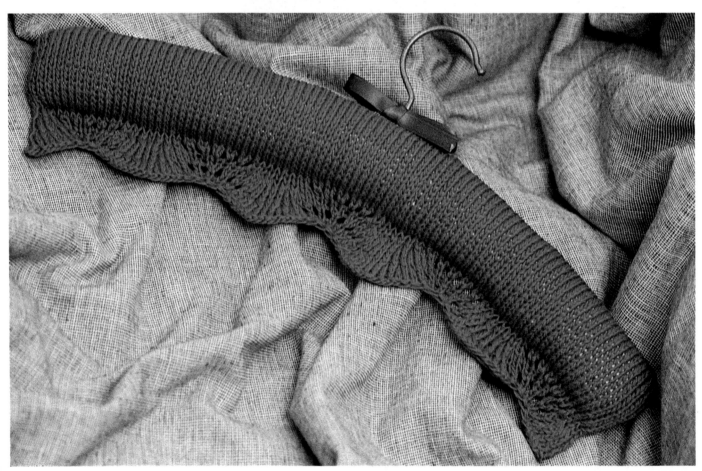

Cottage Tea-cosy

The only possible accessory at the traditional English tea-table, this tea-cosy uses light weight worsted wool to create a country cottage. The scope for alternative colorways is quite wide since your cottage may be white-washed, pink-washed, grey stone or even red brick with a variety of paintwork and roofing. When large areas of color, such as the windows, are being worked, use separate balls. On smaller areas, such as the fence, carry the color at the back of the work (for the fairisle and intarsia methods, see Techniques, pages 10-12).

Front and back
Using No.6 needles and wall color, cast on 77 sts and work from chart, starting with a knit row and keeping in st st. When the roof is worked, dec 1 st at each end of every alt row as indicated. When the roof is complete, bind off.

Sides
Using No.6 needles and wall color, cast on 31 sts and work from side chart, starting with a knit row and keeping in st st. Work both sides the same.

Tab
Using No.6 needles and roof color, cast on 7 sts and work in garter st (knit every row), for 2½in. Bind off.

Lining
Using No.6 needles and whatever colors remain (in stripes if necessary), work the pieces as for the outside of the cosy, omitting the cottage design and casting on

Materials
Light weight worsted wool: **roof and wall color**: 3½oz each; **all other colors**: 1oz of each.
Those small amounts which are left over may be used to work the lining in stripes according to how much you have of each.

Needles
One pair of No.6 needles.

Gauge
Using No.6 needles and measured over st st, 24 sts = 4in.

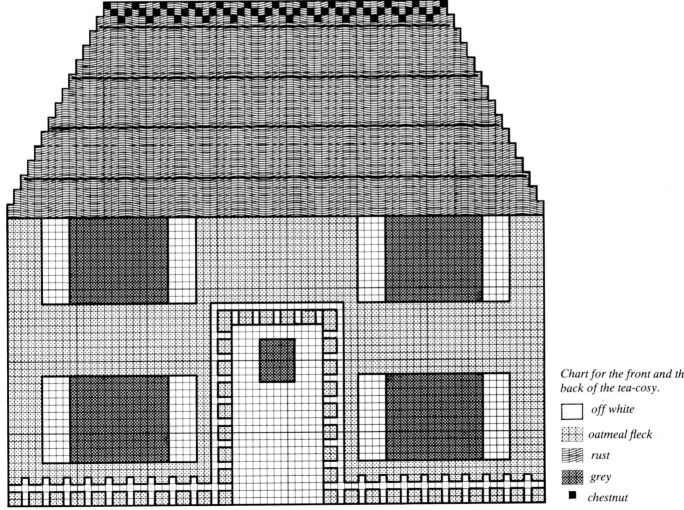

Chart for the front and the back of the tea-cosy.

☐ off white

▨ oatmeal fleck

▨ rust

▨ grey

■ chestnut

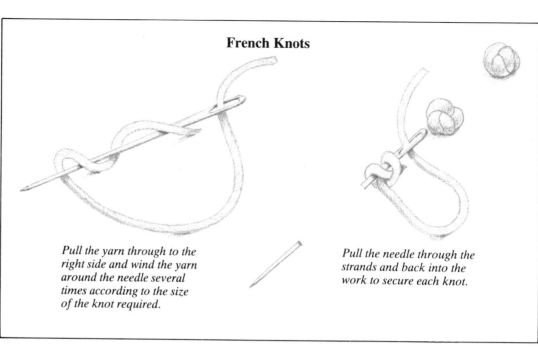

French Knots

Pull the yarn through to the right side and wind the yarn around the needle several times according to the size of the knot required.

Pull the needle through the strands and back into the work to secure each knot.

2 stitches less for each piece so that they will be slightly smaller and fit inside.

Embroidery

This is easier if worked before the finishing stage. The leaves around the fence and trellis are worked in backstitch as are the windows. The door knobs and flowers are French knots (*see* diagram on how to work these).

Finishing

Fold the tab in two and place it between the two roof pieces in a position to suggest a chimney. Work a flat seam along the top of the roof, securing the tab as you do so. Join the sides of the cottage with a flat seam. Join the lining pieces in same manner and slip it inside the cottage. Put a few sts through the two thicknesses at the top of the roof and then overcast stitch the two tog all around the bottom edge.

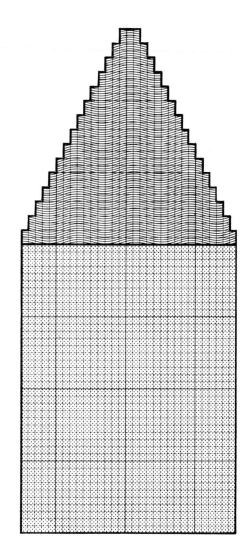

Chart for the side of the tea-cosy.

 oatmeal fleck

rust

Teddy Bear Hot-water Bottle Cover

Materials
3½oz golden-yellow mohair (or any fluffy yarn that knits to gauge). Scraps of heavy weight worsted yarn in bright contrasting colors. Black wool for nose.
Pair of glass eyes for face.
2 gripper snap fasteners.

Needles
One pair of No.8 needles.

Gauge
Using No.8 needles and st st, 20 sts and 24 rows = 4in.

Use up your odd balls of mohair and heavy weight worsted with this bright and cuddly Teddy Bear hot-water bottle cover. During the summer you can use the cover as a nightgown case. Blue and white stripes have been used for Teddy's nightshirt, but random-colored stripes would look just as attractive.

Front
Using No.8 needles and starting with a leg, cast on 8 sts in mohair. Begin with a knit row working in st st and increasing 1 st at each end of the first 3 alt rows (14 sts). Work 7 rows without shaping,* break off yarn and slip these sts on to a spare needle. Rep from beg to * for second leg, turn, cast on 10 sts, work across sts held on spare needle (38 sts). Cont in st st, inc 1 st at each end of the next row, then work even for 2½in, ending with a purl row.
**Change to first desired contrasting color of heavy weight wool and cont as follows:
Row 1: p1, *k2, p2, rep from * to last st, p1.
Row 2: k1, *p2, k2, rep from * to last st, k1.
Repeat these 2 rows twice more, change to next contrasting color and cont to work even in st st, changing colors every 4 rows until you have completed 3 stripes, plus the rib. Change to another contrasting color and begin knitting "Hotty" placing the chart as follows:
First row (RS): A=base; B=contrast for letters.
K4A, 2B, 7A, 2B, 5A, 2B, 5A, 2B, 3A, 2B, 1A, 2B, 3A.
This sets up placement for the chart. Cont following the chart, using the same base color throughout, until it is complete. Change to a new contrasting color and cont in stripes of 4 rows until you have completed an additional 3 stripes. Work 3 rows of the next stripe. **Begin head:** cont in striped sequence, k15 base, k10 mohair, k15 base.
Row 2: (mohair shown as M): k15 base, k14 M, k11 base.
Row 3: k11 base, k18 M, k11 base.
Row 4: k11 base, k21 M, k8 base.
Row 5: k8 base, k24 M, k8 base.
Row 6 and 7: work as for row 5.
Bind off the 8 base sts at beg of next 2 rows. Cont in mohair only, inc 1 st at each end of the next row and the following alt row. Work 7 rows even. Dec 1 st at each end of the next row and the next 2 alt rows. Dec 1 st at each end of the next 2 rows. Bind off 4 sts at beg of the next 2 rows. Bind off remaining 10 sts.**

Back
Work the first paragraph of the instructions for the front. Cont in st st in mohair for another 12 rows. Bind off.
With the first contrasting color of heavy weight wool, cast on 40 sts.
Return to front pattern and work from ** to **.

Arms (Make 2)
Using mohair, cast on 16 sts. Work in st st, inc 1 st at each end of every row until you have 26 sts. Change to first contrasting color of wool and work 4 rows in k2, p2 rib. Change to 2nd contrasting color and cont in st st stripe sequence, inc 6 sts evenly along first row. Work 2 complete stripes, change to contrasting color, work 6 rows in st st. Bind off. With RS of arm facing, fold in half lengthwise and (on WS) sew seams, taking care to match stripes.

Ears (Make 2)
Using mohair, cast on 8 sts. Working in st st, inc 1 st at each end of the next 2 rows (12 sts). Work even in st st for 8 rows, then dec 1 st at each end of the next 2 rows. Bind off remaining 8 sts. Fold ears in half to form a half-circle and carefully sew around seam (WS together). Then, using a back stitch, sew a line around the curved edge of the ear to form a narrow ridge, (*see* diagram A).

This chart should be incorporated into the hot-water bottle cover pattern.

Snout
Using mohair, cast on 8 sts. K 1 row.
Working in st st, inc 1 st at each end of the
next row. Work 2 rows even. Dec 1 st at
each end of the next row. Work 3 rows
even. Bind off.

Nose
Using black wool, cast on 1 st. K5 from
this one stitch, turn, p5, turn, k2 tog, k1,
k2 tog, turn, slip 1, p2 tog, psso. Cut yarn
and tie the two ends of yarn together,
forming a bobble. Attach this bobble to

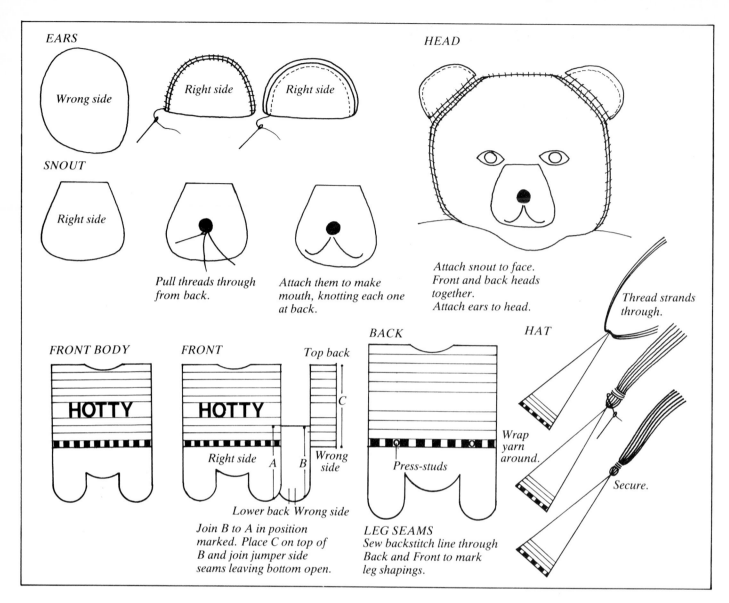

EARS

Wrong side

Right side

Right side

SNOUT

Right side

Pull threads through from back.

Attach them to make mouth, knotting each one at back.

HEAD

*Attach snout to face.
Front and back heads together.
Attach ears to head.*

Thread strands through.

FRONT BODY

HOTTY

FRONT

HOTTY

Right side

A   *B*

Lower back Wrong side

Top back

C

Wrong side

Join B to A in position marked. Place C on top of B and join jumper side seams leaving bottom open.

BACK

Press-studs

LEG SEAMS
Sew backstitch line through Back and Front to mark leg shapings.

HAT

Wrap yarn around.

Secure.

---

the center of the right side of the snout. Use the black ends of yarn to embroider Teddy's mouth (*see* diagram B).

Finishing
Attach snout to face, placing the widest end 4 rows up from where the main face begins. Attach glass eyes either side of the top of the snout. Place front and bottom back on top of each other RS facing and join using a flat seam. Match front and back ribs of sweater and sew up side, shoulder and head seams, taking care to match stripes. Do not attach the back sweater rib to Teddy's mohair bottom half as this should be left open (*see* diagram D) for the hot-water bottle. Sew 2 gripper snap fasteners on the inside of the back rib with corresponding halves on the top of the mohair back body. Carefully pin

and attach ears either side of head and finally, place a neat row of backstitches along the top of the legs (*see* diagram E).

Hat
Using heavy weight worsted wool, cast on 42 sts. Work in k2, p2 rib for 4 rows, change to contrasting color and cont in st st and striped sequence, dec 1 st at each end of every 3rd row. When 3 stripes have been completed, cont dec as before, but using base color only until you have 2 sts left. Bind off. Fold in half lengthwise and join side seams together (RS facing). Turn inside out. Make tassel by threading (6) 4in strands of yarn through the point of the hat, leaving equal lengths on either side. Using one strand, wrap this around the top of the tassel and secure firmly (*see* diagram F).

Acknowledgements

Illustrations by Kate Simunek.
Photographs by Robert Mackintosh.
Styling by Debby Robinson.
Clothing on pages 2, 38, 39, 68, 72, 73 by:
Nigel Preston,
41 Goodge St.,
London W1.
(Phone 01-580 3361 for stockists)